DO NOT REMOVE
CARDS FROM POCKET

LEADERS
AND
LAWYERS

LEADERS
AND
LAWYERS

by
Irene M. Franck
and
David M. Brownstone

A Volume in the Work Throughout History Series

A Hudson Group Book

Facts On File Publications
New York, New York ● Oxford, England

LEADERS AND LAWYERS

Copyright © 1986
by Irene M. Franck and David M. Brownstone

Library of Congress Cataloging-in-Publication Data
Franck, Irene M.
  Leaders and lawyers

  (Work throughout history ; 2)
  Bibliography: p.
  Includes index.
  Summary: Explores some of humanity's major occupations, such as diplomat, lawyer, police, and political leaders.
  1. Occupations—Juvenile literature. 2. Professions
—Juvenile literature. [1. Occupations]
I. Brownstone, David M. II. Title. III. Series.
HF5382.F693 1986   331.7'02   85-27531
ISBN 0-8160-1367-5
Printed in the United States of America.
10 9 8 7 6 5 4 3 2 1

7113253

Contents

Preface

Leaders and Lawyers is a book in the multi-volume series, *Work Throughout History*. Work shapes the lives of all human beings; yet surprisingly little has been written about the history of the many fascinating and diverse types of occupations men and women pursue. The books in the *Work Throughout History* series explore humanity's most interesting, important, and influential occupations. They explain how and why these occupations came into being in the major cultures of the world, how they evolved over the centuries, especially with changing technology, and how society's view of each occupation has changed. Throughout we focus on what it was like to do a particular kind of work—for example, to be a farmer, glassblower, midwife, banker, building contractor, actor, astrologer, or weaver—in centuries past and right up to today.

Because many occupations have been closely related to one another, we have included at the end of each article references to other overlapping occupations. In preparing this series, we have drawn on a wide range of general works on social, economic, and occupational history, including many on everyday life throughout history. We consulted far too many such wide-ranging works to list them all here; but at the end of each volume is a list of suggestions for further reading, should readers want to learn more about any of the occupations included in the volume.

Irene M. Franck
David M. Brownstone

Introduction

The givers, makers, enforcers, and interpreters of laws
and other formal rules of conduct for society are the
subject of this book. *Political leaders* may range from the
absolute ruler, such as a monarch or dictator, to (in
theory) the very citizens of a democratic state. Between
these two extremes are a great many political leaders
who, over the centuries, have had considerable influence
on the complex and sometimes cumbersome legislative
process. Even absolute leaders must share a great deal of
their authority with delegated officials. Even in the most
democratic of governments, people generally surrender
their direct influence on the lawmaking process to their
duly elected representatives.

In early times, the most important official, next to the
ruler, was the *judge*. Literally sitting at the ruler's right
hand as an honored advisor in all matters, the judge had

enormous authority. As society grew more complex, a whole hierarchy of judges was developed to see that the ruler's laws were carried out at every level of society.

Another highly trusted official closely tied to the ruling political leaders was the *diplomat*. For most of history, diplomats were actually members of the ruler's family, or of the aristocratic families most closely associated with the throne. Although today many diplomats are highly trained professionals, rulers still often use close relatives and personal advisors for delicate missions.

In many societies, from early times up to today, it was thought that individuals should go before a judge on their own, without any expert guidance, but only the counsel of perhaps a wise friend or relative. So, many societies tried to do without *lawyers*—even in Greece and Rome the profession developed almost in spite of public preference. Today, however, lawyers are extremely influential members of society, many of them becoming political leaders; though they may be the subject of many complaints, they are regarded as essential for the protection of citizens' rights and freedoms.

Enforcement of the law within the country is delegated to the *police* and other *law enforcement officers*, who may be civil servants, paramilitary officers, or even military personnel. They are a rather recent arrival on the social scene. For most of history, it was felt that the job of protecting private property was a private affair, so the night watch in a city was generally made up of citizens—and later ill-paid substitutes—on a rotating basis. Only in the modern industrialized world, with its large, overcrowded cities, has a professional police force been created. Prisons are also a rather modern invention, so *prison guards* are relative newcomers on the occupational scene as well. *Executioners* have, however, long been employed by rulers and judges handing out harsh and sometimes deadly sentences. A separate force called the *secret police* is often charged with focusing on political behavior in a society, identifying and sometimes acting against people who oppose the government in power.

Various officials also make regular checks to see that the laws (and sometimes informal codes of conduct and morality) are being properly obeyed; they may even take a direct part in carrying out certain laws. Among these are the many different types of *inspectors*—those who monitor foods and drugs, weights and measures, or industrial safety, for example. *Border control officials* are especially charged with checking all people and goods that cross a nation's boundaries.

All of these professions have had enormous impact on society ever since the beginning of civilization. The public decrees and foreign policies of kings demonstrate this without explanation. But even the quieter and unsung heroics of legislators, town councillors, and mayors have had real and lasting effects on the shape and growth of the society we live in.

Border Control Officials

Border control officials are employed to check what comes in or goes out of a country, including people. They try to prevent the passage across their borders of items that are either illegal in themselves or illegal to trade. Such forbidden items are called *contraband*.

Contraband items include drugs, stolen goods, or firearms. Border control officials also oversee the proper collection of taxes, called *customs duties* or *tariffs*, from goods that are permitted to cross the border. For this reason their jobs are usually closely controlled by the governments for which they work.

The earliest forms of border control may be traced to ancient times, when *kings* appointed *soldiers* to inspect travelers and *traders* before allowing them to pass through territories or city limits. In some desert places, as

1

in the narrow Suez crossing between Egypt and Arabia, a group of local people would be set to watch the main crossing points. They would sweep the sand smooth before nightfall; then in the morning, if they found any tracks, they would follow them and apprehend the travelers who had passed through without approval, often to avoid payment of customs duties. In other places, as in the narrow mountain passes of southern Arabia, travelers would be forced to file through a narrow opening, wide enough to admit only one pack animal. That way, the customs officials hoped, no animals would slip by unchecked, and proper duties could be collected on all.

As trade between nations became increasingly common, international rules and restrictions on this activity were passed by governments and enforced by border control officials. Throughout most history these officials were soldiers, or else civilians trained and supervised by the army.

Law enforcement related to international trade began to take on an entirely new significance in modern times. Beginning in the 16th and 17th centuries, countries such as Spain and England embarked on programs to establish favorable *balances of trade* for their countries. A nation's balance of trade is the difference between the amount of goods it buys from other nations (*imports*) and the amount of goods it sells to other nations (*exports*). A favorable balance of trade is one in which a nation sells more than it buys. England and Spain each tried to increase their exports and to slow down imports by placing restrictive tariffs on them. In this way, each country hoped to protect its own manufacturing while bringing hard currency into the nation. This policy, known as *mercantilism*, gained in importance as the Industrial Revolution began to emerge.

As manufactured goods began to be traded across borders with greater regularity, tariffs took on greater and greater significance. Up until the year 1900 the tariffs collected on imported goods represented most of an industrial nation's stored revenue; even today they represent a large portion of it. The earliest tariffs were in the form of payments for the use of trade and transportation highways, ports, markets, and bridges. The officials who collected the tariffs were extremely important because of the large amounts of revenue they took in for the government.

Today, *customs officials* are still responsible for the prevention of smuggling and the collection of custom duties and tariffs. Although in the past most customs officials were soldiers, this occupation has been steadily taken over by appropriately trained civilians, particularly in North America. Such *civil servants* usually enjoy secure and comfortable positions with relatively high social standing. In a great many countries, however, border control is still a function of the military or of civilians trained and supervised by the military.

Emigration is the act of leaving one's country with the intention of settling in another. *Immigration* is the act of entering a new country with the intention of settling

The lot of the arriving international traveler and the customs official is seldom a happy one. (By Ivan Pranishnikoff, from Harper's Weekly, *March 29, 1879)*

there. Immigration and emigration have always been matters of concern to kings and states. The entry and departure of people across borders were always regulated by the regular army and did not pose any special problems until the development of nationalism and the beginning of the Industrial Revolution. It was at that time that increasing numbers of people sought to leave one country for another for religious, political, or economic reasons. Special classes of civil servants or paramilitary officials now act as *immigration* and *emigration officials* of modern states. They regulate the entry or departure of persons at designated ports of entry. They examine applications, visas, and passports, and interview persons to determine their eligibility to cross the border. These officials have the authority to arrest, detain, or deport immigrants. They patrol the border to prevent illegal entries or departures.

Throughout history there has been a significant degree of corruption in this profession, owing to the considerable degree of authority conferred on these officials. Border patrols, notably in some modern Asian countries, have been charged by international human rights commissions with committing numerous atrocities, such as raping women and robbing men in return for approving their passage across borders. The border between the United States and Mexico has caused immigration officials considerable trouble for many years, and some officials have been known to be receptive to bribery. In recent years the profession has generally come under closer observation and tighter control by governments in order to prevent abuses of its power.

For related occupations in this volume, *Leaders and Lawyers*, see the following:

Inspectors

Police and Other Law Enforcement Officers

Political Leaders

For related occupations in other volumes of the series, see the following:

in *Financiers and Traders*:

Merchants and Shopkeepers

in *Warriors and Adventurers* (to be published Spring 1988):

Sailors

Soldiers

Diplomats

The importance of international relations in modern times has brought to the fore the *diplomat*. The word itself comes from the Greek *diploma*, a folded document that acted as the credentials of a government's representative in another country. From the beginnings of territories, there has been a need for official representatives to conduct negotiations between governments. For most of history, however, these international *envoys*, or *ambassadors*, were members of the royal family or high nobility acting as the personal representatives of their *monarch*. The Greek democracies sent representatives called *heralds* to communicate between the various city-states. But none of these constituted a distinct diplomatic profession.

That did not arise until modern times, when power began to reside more in institutions than in single monarchs. Early professional diplomats continued to be drawn from the upper classes, however; if not of noble birth, they had to have considerable wealth. Even at the turn of the 20th century, Britain—whose international empire was a major spur to and model for the development of a professional foreign service—required that applicants for the diplomatic corps have independent incomes.

The Italian city-states, notably Venice, may have been the first to have permanent representatives in other states, especially those with whom they had trade relations. The official working residence of these representatives was often called a *mission* or *embassy*. Diplomats working abroad often had restricted mobility, being required to live in foreign quarters and to travel

Diplomats like those in this first Japanese mission to the United States often had considerable status in their homelands. (By Matthew J. Brady, 1860, National Archives, Records of the Office of the Chief Signal Officer, 111-B-2325)

only where allowed and under watch. In China, for centuries foreign envoys were obliged to wait in the city of Canton until they were allowed to travel a specified route—called the Ambassador's Road—north to the capital. Diplomats in foreign countries often competed fiercely with each other for ranking and special consideration. The more status and influence they could win, the more power they would have in future delicately balanced negotiations. In 1661, diplomats from France and Spain even fought a pitched battle in the streets of London over just such a seemingly insignificant question—which country's diplomat should precede the other's in a royal procession. Often there were touchy questions relating to whether an envoy from a monarch's own family should be favored over one who was not. In consequence, a set of elaborate rules developed over the centuries regarding the relations of diplomats with each other and with the countries in which they serve.

As modern diplomacy became increasingly complicated and important, various levels developed within the profession. According to the 1818 Aix-la-Chapelle agreement, the highest ranked diplomats were the *ambassadors*. (Also included in this category were *papal nuncios* and *legates* who represented the pope and the independent state of Vatican City.) As prime representatives of their own heads of state, the ambassadors were entitled to have access to and negotiate directly with the leaders of the countries to which they were accredited. In the second rank were the *minister plenipotentiary* and the *envoy extraordinary*, and in the third was the *minister resident*; these were all general representatives of their country, without the right of direct access to heads of state. These two ranks were combined in 1963. The fourth rank was the *chargé d'affaires*, whose accreditation was simply to the foreign minister of the country. These ranks, originally agreed upon only by Western European countries, gradually became widely accepted around the world. As the foreign service grew in size and importance in the 20th century, two other ranks were added; these were the *consuls*, who live in foreign cities and help protect their own nations' citizens and business interests there, and other *foreign service officers,* who work at home, not abroad.

Diplomats have traditionally been granted immunity from civil or criminal prosecution in the foreign countries to which they are accredited, though that immunity does not necessarily extend to their private property. The questions of diplomatic immunity are extremely difficult ones, as Britain demonstrated in 1984 when it had to release without prosecution foreign diplomats who had fired deadly shots from within their embassy on British soil. Many countries have complicated the question by using embassy staff members for secret purposes, such as spying. A diplomat who is, for whatever reason, no longer acceptable to a foreign government is labeled *persona non grata* (an unacceptable person) and is generally recalled home immediately.

For related occupations in this volume, *Leaders and Lawyers*, see the following:
   Political Leaders

For related occupations in other volumes of the series, see the following:
in *Communicators* (to be published Fall 1986):
   Messengers and Couriers
in *Financiers and Traders*:
   Merchants and Shopkeepers
in *Warriors and Adventurers* (to be published Spring 1988):
   Spies

Inspectors

Inspectors have usually been *civil servants* hired by *monarchs, emperors,* and governments. Their main duty is to make sure that the laws governing certain activities are obeyed. Although the areas of inspection have changed throughout history, the job has remained very much the same.

The main difference between contemporary inspectors and those of other times lies in the degree of their authority. Inspectors in most periods of history have had considerable power because they were commissioned directly by the *king* or governing body to strictly enforce the law. The laws usually benefited the state directly, so that their enforcement was serious business. An inspector could easily put a dishonest *tavernkeeper* out of business or send a hoarding *grain dealer* to the official *executioner*.

The visit of an inspector was therefore taken quite seriously and a tough inspector could inspire considerable fear in the community.

Inspectors today rarely evoke that kind of fear. Governments are so large now, and there is such a mass of paperwork to be handled, that a poor inspection report may well go unnoticed for long periods of time. At least its impact becomes very indirect, and offenders are very often let off with a warning or a light fine.

Inspectors have always been notorious for their susceptibility to bribery and corruption. As far back as ancient Egyptian times, royal inspectors were known to skim the top off the king's wealth in grains or other goods that were transported under their supposedly watchful eye. Yet there seem to have been enough honest in-

Throughout history inspectors like this wine-gauger have been employed to see that merchants were shipping proper measures—and paying appropriate taxes. (From Ordonnances de la Prévoste des Marchans et Eschevinaige de la Ville de Paris, *1415, Bibliothèque Nationale, Paris)*

Health inspectors were especially important in the days before refrigeration. (By R. Lewis, from Harper's Weekly, September 13, 1873)

spectors in history to give the profession some honor and social status. Even today there is a constant struggle by governments to try to weed out the corrupt inspectors from the honest and trustworthy ones.

Inspectors exist for nearly everything that is regulated by civil law. In the latter Middle Ages and early modern era, inspectors often did jobs that *police officers* would now be expected to do. They patrolled taverns and inns to keep fighting, gambling, and prostitution from spilling out into the streets, where decent citizens might be exposed to such scandalous activities. In some of the leading cities, they were even empowered to fine or jail persons found throwing human waste out of second-story windows during the daytime; it was only permitted to be thrown out of the ground floor entryways (so as not to land on anyone's head) during specified hours of the night.

Some of the areas in which government inspectors now work are weights and measures, taxation, motor vehicles, sanitation, health and safety, food and drug safety, industrial waste, and industrial safety. Other inspectors are hired by industry for such purposes as quality control.

For related occupations in this volume, *Leaders and Lawyers*, see the following:
    Police and Other Law Enforcement Officers
    Political Leaders

For related occupations in other volumes of the series, see the following:
in *Financiers and Traders*:
    Merchants and Shopkeepers
in *Helpers and Aides* (to be published Spring 1987):
    Sanitation Workers
in *Manufacturers and Miners* (to be published Fall 1987):
    Factory Workers
in *Restaurateurs and Innkeepers* (to be published Spring 1988):
    Innkeepers
    Restaurateurs

Judges

Whenever early peoples arranged to settle their disputes peacefully, they did so according to social customs of the times. Typically, they turned to their *political leaders*—chief, king, pharaoh, prince, emperor, or whatever—as the final arbitrator. The political leader had the power to make the laws, interpret them, and enforce them. This authority, and often the social codes themselves, were considered to have come directly from the gods. The leader's role as arbitrator of disputes was critical, since failure to negotiate problems peacefully often resulted in violence, warfare, long-term feuds, and general chaos. Where societies grew large and complex enough so that the leader could not personally handle all such problems, certain powers had to be shared with others. The powers of interpreting and enforcing the law were delegated to the first legal specialists in history: *judges*.

Most early judges were drawn from the priesthood. *Priests* were often the only citizens who could read and write. They were very powerful figures in the political arena, since they were appointed to assist in the performance of duties rightfully the king's, and were seen as protectors of laws believed to have been divine in origin. Although the king retained the final authority over the enforcement and interpretation of the laws of the land, the chief judge or *magistrate* assumed widespread powers as the leader's most important deputy. A chief judge was generally second only to the king in power and prestige, and enjoyed all the status implied by such an association. In some cases, judges were even raised to the level of gods, as kings so often were. The most powerful chief justice in the ancient world was Egypt's *grand vizier*, whose authority occasionally rivaled even that of the pharaoh.

The grand vizier headed a legal system that was fully developed in Egypt by 4000 B.C. "Superintendent of all the works of the King," he typically held an early morning *diwan* (a special type of court proceeding) at the main palace each business day. At this time he donned a gold collar embossed with the symbolic feather of justice, which indicated his holy dedication to the profession—the feather being the symbol of Matt, the goddess of justice. Otherwise dressed in flowing linen robes, the grand vizier was an impressive and imposing figure of authority as he sat in contemplation, weighing the evidence and statements offered in writing by the *defendant* and *plaintiff*. (The plaintiff is the person who brings charges against someone. The defendant is the accused person.) The grand vizier's final judgment was indicated when he handed his gold collar to the successful plaintiff or defendant. The grand vizier usually presided over criminal trials, although he also heard appeals from lower courts. His afternoons were usually taken up by administrative and legislative duties, since he was a full-time deputy of the pharaoh, besides being the chief justice of the courts. Among other things, he also spent some of his time teaching and training others to be judges.

The pharaoh provided beneficial support not only for the chief justice but also for the other justices commissioned to staff the lower courts and to assist the grand vizier. Following the model set by their chief, these lower judges administered justice in audience halls in various cities along the Nile. They kept all records of titles, boundaries, wills, contracts, and legal actions in such halls, and heard cases pertaining to them as well as to other matters within the community. Their cases were recorded by *scribes* attached to the judicial system; these were the earliest *court recorders*. The judges did not hear testimony from third parties, but only directly from the defendant and plaintiff.

Since there were no *lawyers* in ancient Egypt, and because very few people in the general population could read and write, judges had considerable freedom to decide cases in whatever way they saw fit. The following inscription from that period hints at the pomp and grandeur, as well as the power, that Egyptian justices enjoyed:

> As for every act of this office, the chief judge...shall sit upon a chair, with a rug upon the floor, and a dais upon it, a cushion under his back, a cushion under his feet...and a baton at his hand; the forty rolls of the law shall be open before him. Then the magnates [important people] of [the area] shall stand on the two aisles before him, while the master of the privy chamber is on his right, the receiver of income on his left, the scribes of the chief judge at his either hand; one corresponding to another, with each man at his proper place.

The absence of skilled prosecution and defense lawyers may have deprived magistrates of a breadth of perspective that would be available later as the legal professions matured and competent lawyers could be counted on to present varying viewpoints within the same case. Even so, the Egyptian legal system was an abiding institution,

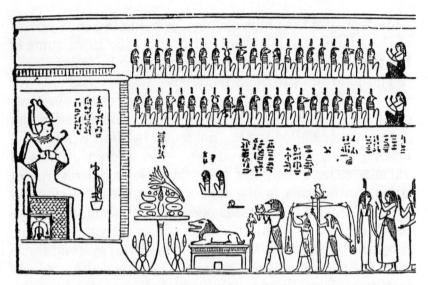

Egyptian judges heard cases and handed down their decisions in the great hall of Osiris. (From History of Egypt, *by Clara Erskine Clement, 1903)*

with professional ethics that tended to make judges responsive to their obligations. A chief judge, for example, admonished an examining judge, in one surviving inscription: "Be quiet while you listen to the words of the petitioner. Do not treat him impatiently. Wait until he has emptied his heart and told his griefs. A kindly judge rejoices the heart." The Egyptians' inherent sense of justice and equality pervaded the profession and prevented its awesome power from being wantonly abused. Moreover, the judges' belief that they were divinely commissioned to carry out the law made them mindful of the seriousness of their responsibilities and of the importance of ruling without self-interest or malice. The Egyptian judges operated their legal system for approximately 4,000 years, until the Romans imposed their own legal system on conquered Egypt.

As in Egypt, Mesopotamian justices had strong ties to the various state religions, and the earliest judges were royal temple priests. But in Babylonia, one of the main kingdoms of Mesopotamia, the judicial system became secularized by the time of Hammurabi, around 1800 B.C. Egyptian law had been only loosely and occasionally written in formal codes, emphasizing instead the mystical, divine source of the law—a source that the justices

Rulers often sat in judgment; here the child-prophet Daniel exposes the false testimony of two witnesses. (By Albrecht Dürer, early 16th century)

were called upon to tap in their legal "interpretations" (actually believed to be more like divine inspirations). The Code of Hammurabi, though, clearly distinguished the secular office of judge in Mesopotamia from its essentially religious counterpart in Egypt.

Since Babylonian law was clearly spelled out, the general population, as well as judges and legal scholars, could easily define the do's and don'ts of the law. Legal codes and legislative decrees were publicly displayed in prominent places, leaving little room for legal interpretation on the part of judges, who acted primarily as *civil servants*. They had far less power or public esteem than the Egyptian magistrates had. Rather than grand courtrooms and elaborate proceedings, they set up streetside courts at the main gate or marketplace of a city; this practice continued in the area for many centuries. Babylonian judges administered justice for the state, simply and directly, quickly and conveniently, by turning to the standard Code of Hammurabi and following it as closely as possible. The king or chief justice was available for appeal in certain kinds of cases. In smaller cities, the local governor or chief magistrate acted as judge, as did the mayor in small towns and villages.

The early Hebrew judges were, like those of Egypt, presumed to have been divinely commissioned and inspired. The Hebraic code itself was, according to tradition, given directly to Moses by God. Hebrew magistrates, then, had only to uphold that holy code in fulfilling their obligations within the community. Their posts were, in fact, even more entwined with the religious system than in Egypt. Judges in the period of Moses were all priests, and trials were held in the great temple-palaces before assemblies of judges—including royal judges like the famous Solomon. The Jews' laws and methods of administering justice borrowed heavily from the secular Babylonian system, perhaps as a result of the Jews' long "Babylonian captivity" during the sixth century B.C. Still, the judges themselves were viewed strictly as ambassadors of God, concentrating chiefly on upholding the religious traditions that solidified and distinguished their community. Some became such leading spiritual as well as legal authorities that their interpretations of law were seen within the broader context of religious prophecy. A notable case in point was the great judge Daniel, once called in by the Babylonian ruler Belshazzar to interpret "the handwriting on the wall," as described in the biblical Book of Daniel.

Many schools of religious law developed in Jewish society. Their membership rolls ranged from just a few followers of a master jurist to as many as 1,200 students at a time. Training went far beyond simple familiarization with set legal codes; it involved philosophical and logical investigations into basic issues of *jurisprudence* (the science of law), which gave a scholarly outlook to the profession. Jewish justices became models for the later intellectual development of the profession, which found full expression first in medieval Islamic courts and somewhat later in the Christian administration of *canon* (church) law.

Graduates from the Judaic legal schools attained the status and title of *master*, or *rabbi*. Although this was only a general designation of one learned in the traditional legal, religious, and cultural tenets of Judaism, many rabbis chose to specialize in legal studies rather than to enter the priesthood or teaching professions. It was they who supplied the staff for the Hebraic judicial system, which operated by a system of apprenticeship and promotion from within. Those who wished to become judges started as *juniors*, or assistants, to a judge. Each judge had three juniors. The judges themselves operated in assemblies called *synhedrions* or *sanhedrins*. In most cities, the synhedrion consisted of 23 judges, each assisted by three juniors, seated on four rising semicircles, with the judges on the highest row. In small villages, the court might consist of only three judges. The Great Synhedrion, which operated not only as the supreme court but also as the legislature for the Jewish people, consisted of 71 judges, also assisted by juniors. Judges moved up through the ranks step by step. Becoming a judge in the Great

More judges than Pontius Pilate, here shown with Jesus Christ, have attempted to wash their hands of the results of their decisions. (By Albrecht Dürer, early 16th century)

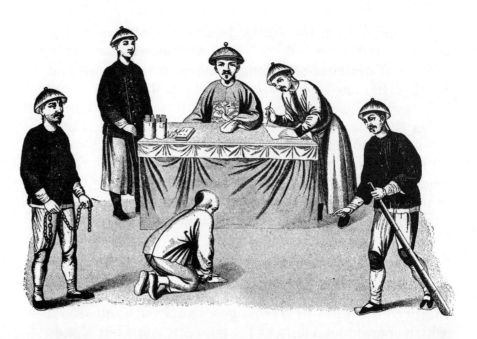

In China, both the discovery process and the trial have traditionally fallen to the judge. (From The New America and the Far East, *by G. Waldo Browne, 1901)*

Synhedrion was the highest achievement of a judicial career. Many judges followed other occupations when court was not in session, acting as teachers and administrators at the schools of religious law. The rules and decisions of these courts were apparently not recorded, since none have survived in written form, but they were passed on orally through the schools and written down later.

Judges were apparently careful not to insist that their decisions were the final word on any subject, for along with their enormous legal authority went the awesome moral responsibility of interpreting divine law. Even though all judges were ordained rabbis, judicial opinions did not automatically convert into law, and a great variety of opinions was allowed. As a result, Jewish law became singularly flexible, and dissent (disagreements) became as important a feature in deciding cases as did concurrence (agreement). Varying judicial opinions surrounding case decisions became the very stuff of learned discussion among Jews throughout their history; it is told of Jesus, for example, that he showed himself an advanced student when at age 12 he argued questions of religious law with the rabbis in the temple. For 2,000 years after the Jews were dispersed from the Near East, the records of their legal cases from this period were the subject of written studies and collections by learned scholars; these served to perpetuate Jewish tradition—even during those periods of history when the Jewish judges could rule only on internal questions of religious law, being subject to the legal practices of many countries in which they found themselves. Forced by alien governments to practice primarily banking and trading, the Jews also developed an extensive set of judicial practices relating to commercial law during this period. Through the processes of review and interpretation, Jewish judges had more to do with lawmaking than any other members of the profession until the beginning of the English common law or case-law systems of justice of much later times.

In the Classical societies of Greece and Rome, judges were virtually stripped of their religious authority and given a second-rate status within the legal systems. In early Greece professional judges played a relatively insignificant role in carrying out legal functions, since the democratic Greeks believed firmly that private citizens, not paid specialists, should initiate and pursue political and legal actions. Magistrates called *archons* were appointed to administer laws, but their main function was to prepare cases for the popular courts, where the cases were actually tried. The judge in a Greek trial was, like the other magistrates and jurors, drawn by lot. Having no special expertise, he acted more like a modern jury foreman or chairman of a business meeting.

Judicial teams usually presided over trials and other legal proceedings. The Athenian Council of the Areopagus, which heard mostly homicide cases, was manned by ex-archons appointed to lifelong terms. The Nine Archons were the chief administrative magistrates of Athens, having jurisdiction over *metics* (resident aliens), recommending revisions of laws, and serving as presiding officers of the law courts. The actions of the law courts themselves, however, resulted chiefly from the decisions of the volunteer jurors (*dicasts*) who, like the archons themselves, were chosen by lot and therefore had little special expertise or knowledge. Jury sizes ranged from 201 to 6,000, leaving the presiding judges with the job of simply maintaining control of so large an assembly, while trying to help them reach some reasonable conclusions about the case at hand. Frequently, the Greeks found it necessary to employ *circuit judges* to visit provincial areas and assist local magistrates. They were, like the other justices, primarily mediators attempting to arrange settlements between hostile parties, although they occasionally exercised their reserved right to impose binding decisions, where necessary.

Roman judges enjoyed somewhat more professional status than their Greek counterparts. Greek magistrates served essentially out of a sense of civic duty. They knew very little about the law, had low prestige, received hardly any money, and were not really professionals at all. They certainly made no claim to divine authority as had Egyptian and Jewish judges. Roman judges, on the other hand, were seen as necessary—if not very important—civil servants and state officials. While making no direct claims to divine authority, they carried out the will of the emperor, who did claim such authority, and at times went as far as to declare their own godhood. Although Roman judges were little recognized for the fulfillment of their often trite bureaucratic duties, they were in a position to go on to greater accomplishments in public life—chiefly careers in politics or legal scholarship.

Roman judges, who held various titles depending on what level they had reached in the judicial system, were primarily public administrators with little or no legal training. As a result, they relied heavily upon the advice of *jurisconsults*, legal interpreters who advised all parties—lawmakers, judges, advocates, plaintiffs, and defendants—in matters of legal procedure and application of the law. Judges and jurisconsults were both drawn from the same high aristocratic class in early Roman times, but the jurisconsult had considerably higher status; the judge's position was merely a stepping-stone toward higher public office and, eventually, to a career as a jurisconsult. At the high point of the profession during Classical times was the office of the *praetor*, who presided over cases heard in the Roman Forum. Heading a panel of some 50 or 60 *judices*, who acted as a jury with the power to deliver both verdicts and judgments, the praetor took on the responsibility of further refining and summarizing their statements. In the final decision, the praetor actually came to interpret and modify the law as well as to merely explain and apply it.

As the administration of the Roman Empire became more complex and bureaucratic, judges were assigned permanent, salaried staffs of trained legal advisors. These staffs eventually undercut the reliance on the aristocratic jurisconsults, who had worked only for honor and prestige. The judges themselves—also once drawn primarily from the aristocracy—held increasingly rigorous, monotonous, and thankless positions. They were obliged to work long days, beginning at dawn and often sitting in session well into the night. They were commonly the objects of verbal abuse, even during trials, and seldom had any power or authority. They usually sat in large teams with co-magistrates, all of whom

In Moslem communities, the qāḍī heard and decided cases without the intervention of lawyers or other professionals. (From Maqāmāt, by al-Harīrī, 13th century, Bibliothèque Nationale, Paris)

applauded or cheered each others' courtroom statements, whether serious or humorous. Cases at the Basilica Iulia, for example, were heard and ruled on by the *centumviri*, formed of four "chambers" of judges. Each chamber, separated from the others, had 60 members—a total of some 240 judges.

A virtual circus atmosphere often prevailed in Roman courts, as throngs of people crowded in for the sheer spectacle and entertainment of it all. Sitting amid the fray, the judge was not only a popular target of jeers and catcalls, but could even be prosecuted by plaintiffs or defendants if he was not careful in making his decisions. When extremely important cases came up, the Senate stepped in to act as the High Court; sometimes even the emperor himself intervened. In all, there was little respect for the regular magistrates, who were no longer drawn from the highest aristocratic classes.

The Late Empire saw actual corruption in the judicial profession becoming commonplace. One outraged observer in the fourth century A.D. remarked that the "doors are now daily more and more opened to plunder by the depravity of judges and advocates who are all alike

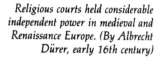

Religious courts held considerable independent power in medieval and Renaissance Europe. (By Albrecht Dürer, early 16th century)

and who sell the interests of the poor to the military commanders." With the whole system of Roman justice about to be toppled, along with the other institutions of the empire, judges were found, at best, to still be generally untrained in law and acting primarily as government functionaries, applying laws that had been made and interpreted by others.

Despite its shortcomings, however, the Roman judicial profession left a substantial legacy, which survives to this day. The simple and functional role of the Roman judge would later set the pattern of development for the profession in the many countries whose legal systems derived from that of the Romans.

In the East, the judicial role developed very early in history and has undergone surprisingly little significant change, even into modern times. Most of the Far Eastern world followed the lead of China in the establishment of judicial systems.

Before the second century B.C., China was ruled by feudal lords. Local lords and nobles administered justice on a community basis, according to custom, in whatever way they saw fit. Then, as a reaction to constant warfare and civil strife, the short-lived Ch'in Dynasty (221-206 B.C.) saw the rise of a group of harsh, almost tyrannical judges; they tightly administered a central, codified law that was imposed on all, regardless of local legal developments or customs. The Ch'in magistrates judged strictly according to the letter of the law, in the tradition of a Chinese school of thought known as *Legalism*.

The chief opponents of the Legalists were the *Confucianists*. The Confucianists argued that laws and punishments were a last resort in social control. More important than laws, they believed, were the careful nurturing of family and clan cohesiveness and responsibility, the proper moral education of the citizenry according to the high social ideals of Confucius, and a strict adherence to the social custom of class privileges and restrictions. If one respected these traditions and morals, thought Confucius, there would be little need for laws, courts, and legal specialists. Apart from the Ch'in era, the Confucianists have, throughout Chinese history, generally dominated the development of justice and its related professions.

Beginning with the Han Dynasty (206 B.C.-220 A.D.), Chinese law drifted steadily toward the ideals of the Confucianists. Nonetheless, a suddenly and vastly enlarged empire necessitated the writing of basic legal codes and some bureaucratic administration of justice throughout the empire and in outlying districts and provinces.

Judges were civil servants employed by the state, and they presided primarily over cases related to public issues, such as the corruption of officials. Private law remained essentially a family and clan matter; individuals rarely brought lawsuits into public courts. This system remained basically unchanged over the next 2,000 years. Since the emperor was the divine keeper of peace and order, any crime or legal difficulty at all reflected badly on his ability to maintain that order. Rather than offend the emperor, magistrates tried to keep the courts clear of cases altogether, particularly petty ones that could be handled otherwise.

To make the legal process more efficient, the Chinese developed legal codes early on, culminating in the T'ang Code of 624 A.D. Magistrates were obliged to stick closely to the code's continuous scale of penalties. Punishments varied widely, depending on the relative social positions of the accused and his victim. Judges were bound to sentence guilty parties to such punishments as strokes of the cane, forced labor, exile, strangulation, or decapitation (beheading). There was little judicial flexibility in such sentencing, since it was dictated by the terms of the code. Judges were basically administrative officials whose main function was to define a crime and then trace it to its correlating punishment in the penal code. Even the biased treatment of various social classes was systematized so that, for instance, it was not up to a judge to decide whether a privileged person could commit suicide rather than be executed; that luxury was already provided for in the T'ang Code. The judge had only to determine whether or not the defendant met the qualifications established by the code.

Chinese judges were generally genteel amateurs, who knew little about law. Even the long-overdue editing of the criminal code, which began in the 18th century, showed little legal insight on the part of the pioneer magistrates involved. As recently as 1956, Dr. Robert van Gulik, an authority on Chinese law, noted that "Copies of the code and other books of legal reference are conspicuous by their absence" at the judicial bench. So ignorant of the law were these pompous civil servants that a special class of lowly legal *secretaries* were employed to do the actual legal research involved in daily casework. These secretaries came to form a hereditary guild centered in Shaohsing, so becoming known as the

Judges often took to their horses, riding circuit to hold trials in a large district. ("The Righteous Judges" by Hubert and Jan Van Eyck, early 15th century, from Classical Picture Gallery, *1897)*

"Shaohsing clerks." They did the detailed work related to cases, and the justices presented the findings as their own.

Since the code was the sole authority in Chinese justice, judicial decisions had no bearing on later cases or on lawmaking. Still, some judges, such as the legendary and celebrated Judge Dee who served as minister of the state sometime between 630 and 700 A.D., became quite active in the cases they undertook. Judge Dee and others did investigative detective work related to their cases and acted as examiners of evidence in the absence of a well-defined or active class of lawyers. Frequently, though, Chinese judges sought easy solutions by simply forcing verdicts through the use of torture and threats, both in and out of court. These methods were well within their authority, and in fact their ruthlessness was officially encouraged. Although judges were commissioned to investigate and initiate cases and to hear complaints routinely on certain days of the month, they were also ordered by the emperor to keep the court calendar as clear as possible, for reasons we have already noted. The extremes to which this official mandate was carried may be seen in the Emperor K'ang Hsi's 17th-century assessment and decree:

> ...lawsuits would tend to increase to a frightful amount, if people were not afraid of tribunals, and if they felt confident of always finding in them ready and perfect justice....I desire therefore that those who have recourse to the tribunals should be treated without any pity, and in such a manner that they shall be disgusted with law, and tremble to appear before a magistrate.

This policy was quite effective. Throughout Chinese history magistrates remained generally cruel, ignorant, and backward. The family continued to be the major source of justice.

The Chinese had great influence on much of Asia, and their legal system became a model for other Asian nations. For example, the Japanese Taiho Code (701 A.D.)

was modeled on the Chinese T'ang Code, and Japanese justices were similarly limited by it. In India, the Laws of Manu, developed between 200 B.C. and 200 A.D., established the rules for legal actions there. Indian judges, however, were generally much more enlightened, creative, authoritative, and prestigious, being drawn from elite social classes and being closely advised by the Brahmin priests.

Islamic judges have, throughout their history, occupied a position in society similar to that of the ancient Hebrew judges. They were believed to have special religious insight based on their relationship with Allah and their understanding of the sacred Koran, written in the seventh century A.D., when the Moslem religion was founded. Like their Jewish counterparts, they were prominent religious and political leaders in communities that barely differentiated between the sacred and the secular, between religion and government. The law of Islamic lands was based on the Koran—itself a book of generally moral rather than strictly legal teachings. The job of the Islamic judges, then, was to translate "Koranic law" into the operation of state and family, as it pertained to the highest public official as well as the meekest individual citizen. This critical task had an enormous effect on the development of Islamic culture.

The *qadis*, the presiding judges of the religious courts, were very influential and highly esteemed figures in Islamic life. Being the supreme executive as well as judicial authority of the land, the qadi was in charge of expounding the fine points of the *Shari'ah* (the "road" or the "true way"; that is, the holy law) for the benefit of all who sat in his court. Despite his power, however, the qadi usually had little knowledge of civil law and kept court proceedings simple and to the point. He was not supposed to have any authority to interpret or modify the Shari'ah, which was thought to be perfect and set. But because the Koran did not always clearly address all questions of civil law, some amount of opinion became necessary in practice. The qadi judged only the most obvious facts in

relation to the most clearly established laws, while an expert known as a *mufti* offered legal opinions. The consensus of legal opinion developed by the muftis helped modify and even create Islamic law—supposedly, only when the Koran was incomplete or vague regarding specific legal points.

The qadi, as the presiding judge of the religious courts, enjoyed apparent power and authority, and therefore very real social esteem; but in practice, his influence on the development of Islamic law was quite limited. Even in the simplest administration of justice, he conceded much of his responsibility to the legal and court clerks known as *katibs*. The court proceedings themselves were kept exceedingly simple, admitting only direct oral pleas and rarely any type of legal representation. The judge's most difficult task in a case lay in establishing the burden of proof—that is, in determining whether the prosecution or the defense was legally bound to prove its position. Once that had been established, the hearing proceeded quickly and directly, with little fanfare and few demands on the qadi's creativity.

In Europe, after the fall of the Roman Empire, the *canon law* of the Roman Catholic church became the supreme authority of the West. No professional judges presided over these ecclesiastical (church) courts; instead, high-ranking priests, bishops, and other clerics expounded biblical law and church dogma as part of their duties.

For centuries, the legal profession itself sank into obscurity. During the long period of feudalism, lords and nobles administered justice in their own petty courts, guided only by local laws and customs. This so-called *Germanic law* was loosely arranged and often spontaneous, bending easily to the whims of the landed gentry and bearing down heavily on the common peasantry. Local law officials, not professional judges, generally acted as both the executive and judiciary branches of local government. These officials, acting as *stewards* for their lords, were typically granted a portion of the fines that they received during sessions of the *hallmote* (local court). The court session itself was quite informal, often being held outside in a field. There was seldom any legal representation of clients. The judge would listen to the clients' oral pleas and to the opinions of *suitors*—upper class citizens and freeholders who owed *suit* (civil service) to the court. Having heard pleas and opinions, the steward-judge made his final judgment based largely on his common (rather than legal) sense and on a consideration of the relative social positions of the parties involved.

During these superstitious times, there developed some kinds of trials that bypassed judicial judgment almost completely. People suspected of committing a crime were obliged to undergo a trial by ordeal—to do something that would normally cause great injury or death, such as walking through fire or pulling something out of boiling water. If they could do so without injury, it was thought that God had demonstrated their innocence. Sometimes the ordeal was not dangerous but designed for "God's will" to be shown, such as being required to swallow bread that had been blessed by a priest; it was thought that a guilty person could not do so without being struck dead or at least ill by God. In practice, many of these trials by ordeal were tricks of illusion, in which those staging the trial—the priest-judges—could arrange the trial so as to show the result desired. Obviously such a system was open to terrible abuses, but it would be many centuries before the church and the lay judiciary would be able to stamp out such practices completely.

In the same period, and sometimes to avoid a possibly fatal trial by ordeal, parties often chose to endure a trial by combat, and fought with deadly weapons. The loser, if not killed in battle, was often hanged or had a hand cut off. Women and elderly men regarded as unfit for battle were represented in such trials by a *champion*, a knight who fought on their behalf. Trial by combat survived for many centuries, though later in a less drastic form, such as dueling. In none of these so-called trials was there scope for careful judicial inquiry into the actual facts of a case. That would revive only slowly over the coming centuries.

As towns developed in the later Middle Ages, municipal (town) justice began to emerge, although for a long time it remained entwined in the feudal system. In the French region of Champagne, for example, a count's cases were judged by the *provost*, who was usually a *burgher*—that is, a solid citizen of the rising merchant class. The provost was granted a commission on collected fines, plus the property confiscated from a convicted party sentenced to death. He had a definite interest in giving preferential treatment to the rich and the landed, since they offered the better gifts and bribes. In his administration of justice, the provost could force confessions by pulling a defendant's teeth, stretching him on a rack, compressing his chest with brick weights, or other means of torture. While torture was used only rarely in the courtroom itself, awaiting trial in the dungeons allotted for that purpose could be a long and painful process. The provost handed out whatever sentences he liked, and they were usually severe—cutting off the hand of a robber, branding a lawbreaker with a hot iron, or flogging children for misbehavior or disrespect. Prison sentences were rare, and it was expected that a judge would provide for the offender's immediate punishment.

The development of both royal and municipal authority made courts increasingly significant. Town courts—presided over by a group of judges, usually including the mayor and several town councillors—primarily heard cases related to commerce and local disputes. It was the royal courts, though, that provided the best opportunity for the growth of a true judicial profession. Royal statutes and decrees were formal and codified in written form. Their authority began to replace that of local customs, since royal decrees applied to the entire citizenry of a whole kingdom. (For a long time, however, *serfs*—not considered as full citizens—were tried only in manorial courts.)

Because of the complicated nature of the new legal codes, trained and better-educated legal specialists were needed to preside over the royal courts. These educated judges were frequently sent traveling throughout the kingdom to deliver justice to all communities, thereby helping the throne to establish a true "law of the land." Royal judges and *circuit judges* (a term that applied particularly to the English traveling justices) helped to consolidate the authority of the crown and centralize its power.

It was in Norman England that magistrates first began their greatest achievement as a professional body. After the Norman Conquest of 1066 A.D., England was left a land without law. The new royal authority sought to establish legal unity throughout the land. Instead of imposing an obscure code of laws on its subjects, however, the crown commissioned a corps of judges to convert the various customs across the kingdom into a body of laws that would be common to all—hence, the term *common law*. Common law was thus based on the decisions of judges, although the judges insisted that they only "declared" into formal law those traditions that had, in fact, already existed. By the 14th century, the body of judiciary decisions had come to be considered as "evidence of law," and it was not much later that it was regarded as actual law, in and of itself. In the process, judges had become the single most important feature of the highly revered British common law system, which is known also as the *case-law system*. That is, the law of the land is based on decisions reached by individual judges on a case-by-case basis. Each judicial decision establishes a *precedent* that will be referred to in similar cases in the future.

British judges became an extremely prestigious group. By 1300 royal magistrates were being chosen from the elite group of *serjeants*—legal representatives trained at the famous Inns of Court. The decisions of royal magistrates were pivotal to the entire legal system and became the basis for the development of modern *jurisprudence* as a philosophy of law. The decisions were carefully recorded and summarized by *juniors* (student lawyers), who observed the courtroom proceedings from special sections popularly known as *cribbes*. The juniors'

Western patterns of justice were often applied to European colonies, here in an Indian jungle. (From History of India, *by Fannie Roper Feudge, 1903)*

summaries of judicial decisions made the annual *Year Books*, which were originally published as textbooks for law students, but in time came to constitute the only written record of the English common law.

Compiled between the late 13th and early 16th centuries, the *Year Books* give an excellent view of the workings of the English courtroom and the central role of the magistrate. A group of judges heard oral pleas from defendants, accusers, and legal representatives in what came to be known as the Court of Common Pleas, where the general public brought their cases to be heard. In the wide array of testimonies heard in these courts, the statements of those highly respected legal representatives called serjeants were given the greatest weight. The chief justices who presided over the hearings even called the serjeants "brother," indicating that they were only a step away from the bench.

The judges were well-versed in all aspects of the law and gave careful consideration to all testimony. Yet they were not above resorting to purely common sense and even personal bias in many crucial points. For instance, it was recorded in one of the *Year Books* that one "Honore, C.J." (Chief Justice) let it be known that "I am annoyed that Grene [one of the lawyers in the case] makes himself out to know everything in the world, and he is only a young man." Later, when asked by a Serjeant Pultney what would become of his plea to the bench if another issue were entered, Honore characteristically replied that: "It will go to the winds as does the greater part of what you say."

British court trials had clearly advanced beyond the old *wergild* system, in which a criminal could buy his freedom, or issues were settled by ordeal or duel. Judges now sought legal proof rather than divine signs to attest to the validity of testimony. Yet, for all his power, the judge was also subject to some serious weaknesses—corruption and manipulation, the former the result of bribery and the latter from threats of violence. These two pitfalls were, of course, inherent in the judges' overwhelming authority to decide cases and hand out sentences and fines. To protect the system from judicial corruption and to protect magistrates from the threats of defendants and their families, two major innovations were instituted. One was the use of *exclusionary rules*, which made the testimony of certain interested parties inadmissible, such as those who might benefit in some way from a court's decision. A corollary to this was the evaluation of evidence according to the probable reliability of the witness. Hence, a judge might only be able to enter a *quarter-proof* for a business associate of a defendant, whereby a complete stranger's testimony might rate as *full-proof.*

The second major innovation was the development of the *jury system*, whereby a small group of the defendant's peers assisted the justice in weighing the validity of evidence and in making the final decisions of guilt or innocence. The jury system made the judge much more of a courtroom foreman in the sense that he no longer sat alone in judgment, but instead directed the flow of evidence and testimony in such a manner that it would be most meaningful and intelligible to the jury as well as to himself.

These protective rules and changes created some checks on the judge's overriding authority to make decisions. The judge's role as creator of law was further undermined by the tendency of Parliament to insist on making formal legal statutes. Magistrates during the 17th-century reign of King James II had quietly supported the monarch's attempts to decrease the legislative (lawmaking) functions of Parliament, the chief legislative body in the Commonwealth. The judges' unwillingness to interfere with royal threats to the democratic achievements of Parliament were regarded by that legislative body as nothing short of a scandal—a scandal that cost the judiciary dearly in terms of its overall stature and its relationship with Parliament. The struggle was manifest in Parliament's endless push for a comprehensive legal code that would lessen the magistrates' freedom to interpret laws and to create laws on their own through the case-law system.

On the other hand, though, English citizens and even Parliament itself have, over the centuries, tended to prefer the common law approach of gradually developing a legal system with each case decision to the *civil law system* (adopted by most other countries) of imposing on society a set of rules that could be changed or modified very little once formally codified. The common law system seemed more flexible and given to growth and evolving maturity than the civil law system of static regulations that allowed judges little freedom. As the great legal scholar Sir Edward Coke put it, statutes were like "raging tyrants," forcing their will upon society for better or worse. But the common law he thought of as a "nursing mother," allowing the natural and healthy development of its offspring (laws) by its guidance and example (legal precedents).

On the European continent, Roman law had been kept alive by the Catholic church throughout the Middle Ages. During the Renaissance, the study and application of its principles received greater attention than they had since the great days of the empire. The revival of interest in Roman law had considerable effects on the development of the legal professions in Europe. The Romans' late emphasis on imposing precise legal codes was reflected in the *Justinian Code*, compiled from 529-353 A.D. This legal code was eagerly adopted by nations throughout Europe. The Roman notion that laws should be made and delivered by the state's leading political authorities was basic to the civil law system, which found its greatest expression on the European continent. With the rise of nation-states came more and better legal codes, as broader systems of justice were needed to replace the old feudal structure of local, manorial, and customary law. Civil law served well the institution of *absolute monarchy*, which was emerging as the new unifying force of the European nation-states. In an absolute monarchy, a single ruler was the supreme authority in all matters of government, including the judiciary. Such absolute monarchs preferred a civil code, because they could set out exactly the laws and interpretations they wished, rather than being dependent on the precedents and differing judgments of various judges, as in the English system.

The position of professional judges under the civil law was a minor one. Their main task was simply to identify and uphold laws assumed to be perfect and thus not in need of judicial interpretation or review. Judges were considered government functionaries rather than legal experts.

In England, the Renaissance also brought a rekindled interest in serious legal scholarship, but scholars there studied English common law, rather than Roman law. As early as the 12th century, British jurists had compiled cumbersome legal glossaries (dictionaries) called *Expositiones Vocabulorum*. These consisted of practical terms of law that judges needed to know. Despite the fact that the glossaries were poorly organized, seldom even arranged in alphabetical order, most judges depended on them, having virtually no other texts or sourcebooks to refer to.

A whole new era of legal scholarship began with the late 15th-century writings of the British magistrates Sir John Fortescue and Sir Thomas Littleton. In his *De Laudibus Legum Angliae* (*In Praise of English Law*) and other works, Fortescue made an ardent plea for the institution of limited rather than absolute monarchies throughout Europe. Littleton's short work, *Tenures*, became important after it was expanded by Sir Edward Coke. Coke's version of *Tenures* became the leading text on English law, until Blackstone's *Commentaries* replaced it in the 18th century. These texts continued to inspire serious legal debates in Britain until the middle of the 17th century, establishing British magistrates as the most scholarly members of their profession.

Legal debates during this era were not just for jurists and judges, moreover; many aroused highly emotional responses in the general population. In 1607, Dr. John

Cowell, a legal professor at Cambridge, wrote *The Interpreter*, a treatise favoring the civil law tradition because it was based on what Cowell believed to be the inherent and divine wisdom of the king's absolute authority. So outraged was Parliament that the book was ordered to be burned in public by the official hangman!

For several centuries, English courts of law were presided over by a *sheriff* (originally called a *shire-reeve*), acting as a royal agent. But by the 17th century, justice in shires and villages was typically administered by a *justice of the peace*, a royal appointee who amassed enormous power as both the judiciary and executive chief of the local area. Most justices of the peace were relatively ignorant of the finer points of the law and frequently had no training at all. Yet they enjoyed considerable social status, not only because of their authority but also because they were drawn from among the gentry. It was assumed that landowners with social standing in the community would be less prone to the sins of bribery and abuse of power than common citizens would. Perhaps more important, the office of justice of the peace was widely regarded as a stepping-stone to a career in Parliament.

For all its advances, the judicial profession remained relatively undeveloped in many parts of Europe before the 19th century. In France, for example, a few royal magistrates presided over lavish palace law courts, while many more poorly trained and underpaid traveling *seigneurial judges* administered common justice throughout the land. They held court sessions anywhere they could—in fields, barns, and the like. Not until 1673 did a royal edict order all villages to maintain regular courthouses, and it was another century before the order was truly implemented.

In North America, the Boston Puritans placed great emphasis on the role of powerful magistrates as leaders of their divine experiment in the wilderness—their exemplary "city on the hill," which was supposed to show the world how God's perfect society operated. The Massachusetts Court of Assistants was composed of eight magistrates, limited only by each other in the same court. These magistrates had theocratic powers—that is, they acted as judges on both secular and religious issues in the new society they hoped to create. Governor John Winthrop wished the legal decisions of these magistrates to constitute law in the "new England," as legal decisions in England itself had over the centuries formed the common law. He feared that if these magistrates set down a formal legal code, it might reflect too much of the character of the land they had left behind. The Puritan magistrates quickly outlawed everything they considered social vices: smoking, playing cards, dancing, and indulging oneself by wearing imported shoes and lace.

But Winthrop's dream was short-lived, and American justices were soon stripped of much of their authority to establish or review law. A low class of poorly trained individuals soon staffed the American courts. In New York, at the end of the 17th century, the chief justice was an ex-soldier with no legal education. In the backcountry, west of Virginia and the Carolinas, a disgruntled 18th-century observer complained of "the malpractices of the officers of our country courts, and abuses that we suffer by those that are empowered to manage our public affairs." In particular, he complained about fees charged by justices for routine procedures.

Despite the abuses and incompetencies of professional judges, the need to centralize the authority of emerging nations led to an ever-growing reliance on their services—and so to their steadily growing responsibility and power. In time, the increasingly complex world of commerce and trade demanded better training for judges. Those who presided over maritime law courts were among the most proficient and specialized of their profession. Because the Colonies were so dependent on their overseas connections with England, the appointment of justices to these courts became a leading political issue in pre-Revolutionary America. (The most powerful of all justices in 17th and 18th century America and England were *naval commanders*, who enjoyed absolute judicial and executive powers aboard warships.) In the expanding backcountry county courts a class of judges called *commissioners* so completely monopolized jurisdictional and political authority that neither governor nor council were needed, as they were elsewhere in the Colonies. A commissioner's chief officer was the *clerk of the court*, who received and recorded the court fines that helped pay the salaries of judges and others who worked in the courts.

The judicial profession changed during the Enlightenment, as the concept of *natural law* began to replace that of the *divine right of monarchs*. Essentially, this philosophical trend reflected an increasing confidence in the ability of people to use reason to create ideal societies. Through the use of human reason, Enlightenment scholars believed, the great laws of nature might be revealed and applied to society. This idea was in sharp contrast to the older view that monarchs alone could know—through divine revelation—what was best for society. The political ramifications of so revolutionary an intellectual movement were very important. For the judicial profession, it meant that wherever powerful monarchies were giving way to representative and parliamentary forms of government, the public welfare would be protected less and less by royally imposed legal codes and more and more by judges deciding everyday cases and actually creating common law, while reviewing and sometimes modifying formal statutes.

British magistrates were at the forefront of this new movement, which greatly enhanced the power and status of the judicial profession. The movement flourished in Britain not merely because the nation was more receptive to the ideas of the Enlightenment, but also because it was the scene of the first steps of the Industrial Revolution. In the new industrialized world, society became complex enough to demand a true and full professionalization of the legal occupations; and the flagrant abuses committed by the rising class of capitalists made social reform necessary. The fact that England was the leader of the common law world meant that Britain was the natural place for the judicial profession to meet the new challenges head on; and so the "rights of man" gradually became important considerations to British magistrates.

But social reform was not the natural goal of common law judges. For a long time, "court-justice" was a term mocking the disreputable *trading justices*, who administered the law purely for the protection of their own personal and business interests. One contemporary declared that these "were men of profligate lives, needy, mean, ignorant, and rapacious, and [they] often acted from the most scandalous principles of selfish avarice." In the second half of the 18th century, Henry Fielding, the first salaried chief magistrate at police headquarters in Westminster, established the authority of the police magistrate to intervene in instances of social abuse. In a time when industry was turning life in London upside down, Fielding made the magistrate at Bow Street (where police headquarters were located) the champion of the new and downtrodden laboring class. The Fielding tradition of social reform was quickly established, and trading justices virtually disappeared. Judges were soon fighting such things as child labor and apprenticeship abuse, and they struggled to control general disturbances such as gaming houses, cockfighting, and certain theatrical exhibitions.

It was no easy task, however, and sometimes the authority of the judiciary was no match for the will of the mob. Consider, for instance, the time when a committee of justices was called on to end the abuses of "sanitary nuisances"—dealers in alcoholic beverages. An official act initiated by the Middlesex justices to prohibit the retailing of British spirits proved totally unenforceable as British courts, overwhelmed with unpopular cases related to the act, were filled with perjuring, profit-seeking informers. The following account illustrates the utter powerlessness of the court justices in this instance:

> The perjuries of informers were...so flagrant and common, that the people thought all informations malicious, or at

least, thinking themselves oppressed by the law, they looked upon every man that promoted its execution as their enemy, and therefore now began to declare war against informers, many of whom they treated with great cruelty and some they murdered in the streets. By their obstinacy they at last wearied the magistrates, and by their violence they intimidated those who might be inclined to make discoveries, so that the law...has been now for some years totally disused, nor has any man been found willing to engage in a task at once odious as endless, or to punish offences which every day multiplied, and on which the whole body of the common people, a body very formidable when united, was universally engaged.

To many authorities, the French Revolution of 1789 represented a general threat to the civilized world and, particularly, to its ruling classes. In response to the violent overthrow of the ancient régime in France, British magistrates at the end of the 18th century came to be looked upon as guardians of law and order and protectors of the established socio-political structure; so much so, in fact, that they became downright repressive and reactionary. The laboring class, now seen as associated with the new democratic reforms in France, became the targets of the magistrates' efforts to maintain an orderly structure in society. Workers were blamed for the increasing class tension in the new urban areas and were likened to the unruly mobs that had stormed the Bastille. In the industrial centers, magistrates became so independently powerful that they held lifelong posts and could be removed from office only by the action of Parliament. In the first half of the 19th century, they came to represent not only judicial power, but an actual class supremacy through the abuse of their authority. Working class citizens were often seen as conspiring to overthrow the established order and were made the scapegoats and victims of the courts. So honorable a statesman as William Pitt defended such abuses of authority when he declared that "the judges would have been highly culpable if, vested as they were with discretionary powers, they had not employed them for the present punishment of such daring delinquents and the suppression of doctrines so dangerous to the country."

In reality, most magistrates who worked so diligently to oppress the working classes had a more immediate objective and interest. Most of them were, themselves, manufacturers and capitalists, against whom laborers were trying to air grievances. One Colonel Fletcher of Bolton, for instance, was a county magistrate who, along with his cronies on the bench, imprisoned miners whose strike had threatened the operation of his coal mines. *Government inspectors* visiting factories at Wigan in 1828 found that the labor reforms decreed by the Factory Acts had gone completely unheeded. In questioning why, they learned that every single county magistrate was a manufacturer who had disqualified himself from hearing such cases to avoid a quarrelsome conflict of interest. The result was that, for all practical purposes, the Factory Acts did not exist at Wigan.

In another district it was discovered that the only two justices on the bench were both *iron-masters* with nearly 5,000 employees each. They were in charge of trying this considerable laboring population for offenses against themselves, often in response to complaints formally lodged by themselves or their agents. Such justices frequently hired informers and *spies* to offer false testimony against workers, even though the spies themselves were usually ex-convicts or derelicts. Reforms in the courts of England eventually began to mend this situation. Parliament finally responded to the cries of the working class and appointed more impartial and competent magistrates to the bench

In North America, meanwhile, judges suddenly achieved a political significance far beyond that of their colleagues anywhere else in the world. In a time when *constitutions* were being drawn up throughout the industrialized world, as sources of law even more stable and ultimate than legislation and statutes, American justices were awarded (by the principles established in *Marbury v.*

In some European countries, judges and lawyers have continued the tradition of wearing wigs in the courtroom. (Advertising woodcut for Oonagh; or, The Lovers of Lisnamona, *London, 1866)*

Madison, 1803) the power to review all legislation in light of the United States Constitution and its heralded Bill of Rights. This gave Supreme Court justices a power that impinged on the authority of the legislature (Congress) itself. Constitutional and judicial review gave American judges enormous power and prestige. They were quickly established as the leaders of the legal profession, and extremely powerful figures in government.

Elsewhere the authority of judges was carefully restricted. The civil law countries on the Continent and elsewhere were often highly suspicious of any flexibility in their legal systems and did not give judges a very significant role. Given rigid legal codes, the job of the judge was still simply to decide which statute to apply to which case and then to see that the law was carried out appropriately and to the letter. The judicial function was, in short, to centralize the authority of the state rather than to establish an ongoing review of legislation. Civil law judges, then, had much less professional clout than their common law counterparts and were essentially administrative functionaries. They berated common law judges as profiteering and greedy, and the principle of *stare decisis* (the basis of judicial decision-making) was deemed ludicrous.

Civil law magistrates first became significant with the rise of modern nation-states. In the 18th century, Cesare Beccaria, the eminent reformer and scholar of criminal law, gave a classical defense of the civil law system: "Only the laws," he argued, "can determine the punishment of crimes; and the authority of making penal laws can reside only with the legislator, who represents the whole society united by the social compact." Even more directly he stated that "judges in criminal cases have no right to interpret the penal laws, because they are not legislators," and that "the disorders that may arise from a rigorous observance of the letter of penal laws are not to be compared to those produced by the interpretation of them....When the code of laws is once fixed, it should be observed in the literal sense, and nothing more is left to the judge than to determine whether an action be or be not conformable to the written law."

Beccaria's thoughts were taken to heart by those who likewise deplored "the despotism of this multitude of tyrants," referring to common law justices. They determined to institute laws that were as clear as they were perfect, since judicial interpretation was considered the result of the obscurity of laws. Moreover, as Beccaria noted, such clarity was seen as keeping the general public free from becoming "necessarily dependent on a few, who are interpreters of the laws, which, instead of being public and general, are thus rendered private and particular."

The deplorable "few" who made fortunes as "interpreters of the law" were effectively immobilized by the establishment of state legal codes and constitutions. Yet even in the civil law tradition judicial review was usually unavoidable at some level, since laws could not be either perfect or perfectly clear. In many countries, *appellate judges* were given special authority to review both primary evidence and law. In France, magistrates appointed to the Tribunal of Cassation were empowered to interpret the constitution as well as laws; in Germany, Italy, Austria, and Switzerland, the same special privilege was granted to judges of the *constitutional* or *revisionary courts*. Usually, justices of the *cassation* and constitutional courts command great respect as the leaders of their profession. While their decisions have no formally binding authority, they serve as models for decisions in the lower courts. Their reviews have traditionally been issued through unanimous opinion, since to issue dissenting or separately concurring ones (as is common in the United States Supreme Court) is thought to be unethical because it demeans the law. There has been, however, a recent trend toward the publication of dissenting and separate opinions by constitutional court justices.

In the 20th century, the judicial profession has grown continually in prestige and power. It has lost most of its religious and church associations, even in the Islamic

The folksy hometown judge is a staple of American lore. (From Gems From Judge, *1922)*

world, where closer ties to the West and the rise of commercialism have given rise to secular *mazalim* courts, whose justices preside over criminal, estate, and commercial cases. The Shari'ah law and the once enormous authority of the qadis have generally given way to civil law-type legal codes in all but the most orthodox Islamic countries. In India and Pakistan, magistrates have even been awarded the privileges of review and interpretation within essentially case-law systems of justice. Judges in many civil law countries have been given the powers of constitutional review since World War II, particularly in Latin America and Japan. Still, in many cases the courts hold such power only theoretically. In both Chile and Japan, for example, two countries where the judicial profession has supposedly taken great strides, only a handful of review decisions have actually been handed down. *Dictators* and military *juntas* around the world often assemble and dismantle courts of justice at will, as Juan Perón did in Argentina.

Judges in the Soviet Union have also been widely used as political tools by the state. In 1922 Lenin created the watchdog office of *procurator-general*, which differs little from the *procuracy* of Czarist Russia dating back to Peter the Great. The procurator is given "general supervision" of the courts and carefully watches over judges and their decisions to make certain that they remain within the scope of state policy and intent. *Arbitrazh* (arbitration) tribunals hear complaints against the state's economy, and authorities presiding over *comrades' courts* impose the will of the state on factory, farm, and even apartment collectives.

Judges in the civil law countries of Europe and Latin America are beginning to receive better educations and training to go along with the modest increases in prestige and authority that their offices have achieved. These changes have begun to create a new image that may soon prove false the famous French judicial maxim that is translated: "To be a judge, it is not sufficient to be a fool: one must also be worthy." Still, civil law judges have completely separate training and career paths from lawyers, who are more important figures in the courts, especially the lower courts. Only those without ambition, seeking secure and routine jobs, usually apply for judgeships. They are at the bottom of the legal ladder in terms of salaries, political influence, and power.

The most powerful and elite judges in the world continue to be those of the common law world, particularly the United States. There, generally only the finest and most experienced lawyers may gain positions on the benches of trial, juvenile, family, traffic, and probate courts at either local, state, or national levels. The justice of the peace remains a highly esteemed and influential position in England, while in the United States it is of little significance and is usually held by lay persons, often volunteers. By far the most powerful justices are those of the Supreme Court in the United States and those of the High Court in Great Britain. The latter, although no longer necessarily of aristocratic birth, still wear robes and their traditional wigs while on the bench (except in the summer heat) to indicate their lofty status. In modern times, as women have gained access to higher education, many women lawyers have gone on to be judges, though women still form a small proportion of the judiciary as a whole.

Perhaps the greatest issue confronting the contemporary Supreme and High Court justices revolves around their social and political influence. Since 1945, they have taken increasingly bold initiatives in judicial review and interpretation, which have brought them into direct conflict with the legislative bodies charged with making laws. This development has earned justices the scorn of many a conservative legislator who complains bitterly of their unprecedented powers of "creative interpretation." Many critics argue that judicial decisions are often based on general sociological concerns, such as the rights of minorities, rather than the actual dictates of "the law." Such critics question whether judges hand down decisions based on what *is* or what *ought to be* (in their personal opinions) the law. The power struggle between the judiciary and the legislature over interpretation and creation of law is a long-term one and will have profound implications for the future of democratic society.

For related occupations in this volume, *Leaders and Lawyers*, see the following:
  Inspectors
  Lawyers
  Police and Other Law Enforcement Officers
  Political Leaders

For related occupations in other volumes of the series, see the following:
in *Communicators* (to be published Fall 1986):
  Clerks
  Scribes
in *Financiers and Traders*:
  Bankers and Financiers
  Merchants and Shopkeepers
  Stewards and Supervisors
in *Scholars and Priests* (to be published Fall 1987):
  Priests
in *Warriors and Adventurers* (to be published Spring 1988):
  Robbers and Other Criminals
  Sailors
  Spies

Lawyers

No lawyers argued when Hammurabi formed his code of laws or King Solomon made his famed judgments. In most early societies, and indeed in many societies into modern times, individuals were expected to plead their own cases before a *judge* or *magistrate*. Any additional pleading or counsel was to be provided by the head of the family or kin-group, not by a professional legal advisor. The interpretation of laws and the administration of justice were carried out by religious, military, and court officials acting as judges, but there was no special class of legal advocates or advisors—what we would call *lawyers*.

The beginnings of the legal profession can be found in Classical Greece. The democratic Greeks mistrusted legal experts, holding to the old idea that a person involved in a lawsuit should be advised by a relative or neighbor. All citizens of a democracy were expected to be active, knowledgeable, and well-rounded, so representing oneself before the law was considered a basic requirement of citizenship. However, the Greeks brought so many lawsuits against each other that the legal code became increasingly complex. Moreover, the nature of the trial system put the uncounseled citizen at an increasing disadvantage.

Athenian courts were presided over by the so-called *Heliastic jurors*, a body of volunteer citizens and elders. The jury was nonprofessional and large—somewhere between 200 and 6,000 jurors at a given trial. Paying little heed to judicial or legal precedents, these citizens' courts were much influenced by powerful speakers. As a result, people bringing suit began to turn to powerful speakers to act as *advocates* or *synegoros*, speaking on their behalf before the court. These orators used emotional appeals rather than sophisticated legal interpretation to win the sympathies and favorable decisions of the jurors. They even went so far as to hire groups of *dicasts*, professional criers who would applaud, laugh, cry, or protest on cue. As a result, the Athenian courtroom had a rather wild and loose atmosphere with large teams of volunteer jurors trying to sort out the tear-jerking accounts of the defense from the wild accusations of the prosecution—both delivered by orators skilled in the arts of persuasion and dramatic technique. It is not surprising that the advocate was thought of as a bit of a shyster.

The state, too, employed public advocates to plead its case in national matters, ranging from suits between cities over ownership of an island to the defense of an Athenian athlete accused of a foul in the pan-Greek Olympic games, a case surely involving Athenian honor. However, the public mistrusted advocates in cases between individuals, feeling that the orators gave their clients an unfair advantage in court.

Advocates were supposedly barred from accepting fees for their advice and oration, but the prohibition was widely disregarded. These payments only increased the

The white scroll with an official red seal may mark this as a young law student and his wife. (Museo Nazionale, Naples, from Pompeii)

public distrust of advocates, who were accused of greed in accepting payment for services that should have been offered free to friends and neighbors in a spirit of mutual helpfulness. The Greeks even tried to forbid any individual from acting as an advocate more than once in his lifetime, but too few people were then available to act on the state's behalf, so the law was not enforced. Public advocates sometimes worked in teams of 10 or so members, with the chief advocate being paid a small fee and the rest serving as volunteers.

While public advocates worked on the state's behalf through the Classical period, personal advocates were so widely mistrusted for their cleverness that their presence in a case between individuals became counterproductive. The use of advocates had another disadvantage: under Greek law, only firsthand testimony could be given. Since the advocate was supposedly speaking on behalf of the client, the client was unable to speak and give evidence that might not be available from anyone else.

Some orators ceased to appear in public as advocates and, instead, adopted the profession of *speechwriter,* or *logographos*. These speechwriters constituted the only distinct body of professionals connected with the Greek court system, all other participants being, to some extent, amateurs. The speechwriters were a small select group. The names and speeches of hundreds of orators have come down to us from Classical Greece, but a small group of speechwriters—perhaps only 10—was responsible for all those surviving orations.

Unlike advocates, who needed only to deliver ringing emotional speeches to sway the court, speechwriters developed considerable legal expertise on the basis of their specialized work. They were often consulted by clients regarding a proper course of action even before any lawsuit had been initiated.

Even though the speechwriters did not actually appear in court, they still faced public prejudice against experts. This forced them to conceal not only their legal knowledge but even their involvement in a case. They were virtually ghostwriters, attempting to frame a speech so that it fit the person who was to deliver it, giving a convincing appearance of an extemporaneous speech. Failure to give this impression left the client open to the charge of undemocratically receiving expert help, while his poor opponent knew no more about law than what was posted on inscribed slabs in public places. Clients were generally inexperienced orators and merely memorized their speeches and recited them by rote. Most clients were not talented enough to modify the speeches once they got into court in order to meet effectively the arguments of the opposition. Consequently, the measure of a speechwriter's skill was the accuracy with which he anticipated and prepared a speech against the opponent's position. Feelings ran so high over these matters that some speechwriters were criticized or even charged in court for exposing secrets of a defense.

Advocates and speechwriters were both typically upper-class citizens. Some advocates sought a more prestigious vocation by turning their oratorical skills toward the business of political leadership. Many advocates took to speechwriting when turns of fortune required them to earn their living by fee-paid work. Demosthenes, for example, is traditionally supposed to have entered the field of speechwriting after turning to a speechwriter himself for help in recovering his inheritance, squandered by corrupt guardians. Later, he used his oratorical skills in the political arena.

Speechwriters who moved on to what they regarded as higher types of oratory often came to regard their earlier efforts as rather shabby and disgraceful. They sometimes played on the conflicting views of their work, as Demosthenes did in a speech for a client against Lacritus, a speechwriter defending himself:

> Lacritus the defendant has not come into court relying on the justice of his case but knowing perfectly well what has been done by himself and his brother in the matter of this loan, and considering that he is clever at speaking and can easily provide arguments for a bad cause. He imagines he can mislead you as he pleases. This is his profession, and he asks money and collects pupils, engaging to instruct them in these very things.

Like all other parts of the Greek political system, the judicial processes were all in the hands of lay citizens, chosen for their positions by lot for limited terms. Since there was no one person in charge of bringing legal action on behalf of the state, the state had to rely on its citizens to bring such actions—to act in the capacity of what would later become the *public prosecutor* or *district attorney*. While some citizens were active in this area as a public service, their numbers were too few, so the state began to offer a percentage of the monetary fines recovered in certain kinds of cases to the person who brought the action before the public courts, especially for crimes against the public treasury.

As a result, there developed a group of individuals who made a living by bringing actions and collecting fines. These people were called *sycophants*, a word that literally meant "fig-shower," named so because the accuser generally waved his hand in the gesture of contempt called a *fig*—the hand in a fist, with the thumb between the second and third fingers—as he brought the charges before the people's court. Unfortunately, this system of bringing charges was open to widespread abuses, and many of the successful sycophants began to increase their income by blackmail, demanding and getting "hush money" from citizens threatened with legal action.

Participants in a trial crossed rather easily back and forth from defense to offense. For example, in Xenophon's *Memoirs of Socrates*, Socrates advised his friend Crito, who was being bedeviled by sycophants, to hire someone to protect him. Accordingly, Crito hired Archedemus, who not only defended his patron but went on the attack so successfully that some of the sycophants themselves paid "hush money" to be free of his charges. The Greeks attempted to stop the practice of indiscriminate accusations by requiring that certain types of suits be carried through to their conclusion, without the option of

Throughout history, lawyers have been accused of defending unjust cases and using shrewd tactics and delays. (By Jost Amman, from The Book of Trades, *late 16th century)*

dropping the suit or compromising; if the accuser failed to obtain at least one-fifth of the jury's votes, he would pay a fine and be unable to bring a similar suit in the future (although he could always hire another to do so). While not all public prosecutors were corrupt, the public's view of the group is clearly seen in the variety of meanings the word *sycophant* has had in history: *false accuser, blackmailer, rogue,* and therefore a parasite, by which we eventually came to the term's modern meaning, *flatterer.*

While most Greeks remained skeptical of legal experts, some recognized the growing need for a legal profession. Socrates often criticized the practice of leaving government in the hands of amateurs, while specialists were routinely consulted in other areas, such as shoemaking. Indeed, at Socrates' trial, which led to his death, one of the charges against him was that he advised people to consult legal experts, rather than relatives and friends, thereby causing young men to have a lower estimation of their elder relatives. But while experts such as speechwriters were condemned in public, people in legal difficulty wasted little time before soliciting the aid of such specialists.

Following the Greek penchant for oratory, the early Romans had a distinct class of advocates operating from at least the second century B.C. It was during this time that Cato described a lawyer simply as "a good man skilled in speaking." The Roman advocates were experts in public speaking rather than law; they knew only enough law to allow them to understand advice from legal experts. Many of these orators rejected legal knowledge on principle, regarding it as fit only for dull minds and likely to spoil the rhetorical flourishes that characterized the successful advocate. One commentator, Q. Mucius, remarked: "Never yet have I seen the fine furniture of legal science among the household goods of an advocate." Advocates of this time were drawn from the highest, or *patrician,* class; they worked for honor, not pay, regarding it as part of their responsibility to represent others less well-placed than they.

These advocates were the "stars" of the early Roman legal system, having great power to sway the lay jurors who decided cases. The Roman writer Tacitus describes the kind of popular celebrity enjoyed by an advocate of the time:

> Just look...at the imposing retinue of clients that follows you when you leave your house!...Are there any to whom the plain man in the street, our citizens in their working-clothes, more frequently point as they pass by, saying "There goes So-and-So?" Visitors also and non-residents, as soon as they set foot in the capital, ask for the men of whom in their country-towns and colonies they have already heard so much.

Advocacy was often the start of a great public career, in which legal and political matters were closely inter-twined. For a boy to put on the toga of a man and begin a career as an orator was as honorable as to be a soldier, and many, including Cicero, went on to become great statesmen.

Most patrician lads were taught early how to plead cases in court so that they might be in the position to enter a lucrative and prestigious career in public life. By the age of 17, after a boy had received the white tunic of manhood, he could be offered to the public as a full-fledged lawyer. If he was fortunate, and if his family had the right connections, he might enter the scene with the sponsorship of a noted lawyer or politician. If not, he would take on those cases that afforded him the greatest possible public exposure, so that he might gain a solid and identifiable reputation. If nothing else, the aspiring young advocate would make sure to enlist himself in the student rolls of the great teachers and masters of law, thereby gaining some of the master's grand reputation simply by association. What he might actually learn about the law from such an experience was probably minimal, except for the lessons in legal procedure that were learned merely by observing the elders performing in court.

There were no law schools at this time, and the closest thing to formal learning came from the review of Greek public speaking manuals employed by speech teachers, or from the teachings of the *jurisconsults*, the legal experts who often had more of an academic than practical interest in the law. The first professor of advocacy was Quintilian, who in the late first century A.D. began to lecture on his art to students who came to him from all over the Roman world. Aspiring young lawyers made it their business to acquire a knowledge of Roman legal statutes, social customs, and the legal decisions handed down by the most authoritative *praetor's* courts. Beyond this, they might study pertinent textbooks and treatises on law, logic, and rhetoric (public speaking). But the most important components of their training—which was seldom academic, but rather "on-the-job"—were the strict observance of proper and established legal procedure and, most of all, the art of rhetoric.

There was an enormous emphasis on practical methods to win cases, but little concern for the actual structure, logic, history, or interpretation of the law. The most popular teachers of law were those who focused on practical matters, rather than more penetrating questions concerning the nature of the law itself. The renowned Quintilian, for example, was best-known for his highly profitable courtroom advice. For instance, he astutely recommended that the advocate, once he had listened to a client, play the part of his legal opponent and that he should examine closely all evidence beforehand, so that he and his client would not be embarrassed in court by materials that were not what they were said to be.

Clearly, lawyers were primarily concerned with the practical tasks at hand. This was not simply because of their training—which was often so poor that many a practicing advocate barely even knew the law as stated, much less the implications of it. More to the point, most lawyers primarily represented their own and their families' concerns. This self-interested protection of their own estates and legal claims was what had led many to become public advocates in the first place—and the same practical-mindedness often continued throughout the course of their careers. The desire for public office was also a chief motivator for many a patrician advocate. As a result, they were commonly much more interested in making emotional oratorical appeals to win public attention and acclaim than they were in interpreting legal clauses or carefully considering facts and evidence on hand.

It is no wonder that the advocates who pleaded cases in court met with considerable ridicule and scorn. Criticism was not so harsh in the early days of the empire, when advocates rarely demanded fees—although they did "graciously" accept gifts. More obnoxious than their garnering of presents, legacies, and publicity was the way that they went about performing their duties. Their cases were delivered before the tribunals in the form of pretentious and long-winded speeches, which often wandered far from the point at hand. It was not unusual for an advocate to take a full two hours just to introduce his views, before either witness or adversary were even heard from. Such displays of vanity and ambition jammed the Roman courts to the point that Augustus finally had to grant the use of the Forum itself for the trying of cases. The courts were forced into session 365 days a year for the hearing of criminal cases and over two-thirds of the year for the hearing of civil cases.

But the very excesses of the Roman courts provided colorful entertainment for crowds of spectators always on the lookout for an amusing way to pass the day. Advocates used trained voices, broad gestures, and even patterned choreographies to plead their cases. The courtroom was truly their stage, and they were the grand performers. They even hired their own professional applauders. These were called *supper-praisers*, because their timely clapping and praisings as members of the courtroom audience earned them their daily meals, paid for by the grateful advocate who employed them. Those lawyers who could not afford teams of applauders would try to muster

With their wigs, long gowns, and righteous airs, lawyers like these were often ridiculed. (From Punch, or The London Charivari*)*

enough friends and family to give a noticeable show of support. One contemporary lawyer, noting the great dependence of advocates on the rabble-rousing applauders who gambled and played games in the halls and yards during adjournments, observed to his comrades: "It is all over with our profession."

It was far from over for the profession, of course, but a state of decline had set in, particularly as lay juries began to disappear, and, along with them, whatever public acclaim had been given the advocates. While advocates continued to represent their clients before magistrates, they were no longer celebrities. In the Classical period, between 27 B.C. and 305 A.D., more of them were young men drawn from the middle strata of Roman society, aiming to raise themselves socially. These new advocates, not as likely to be independently wealthy, often demanded and expected a fee, although in early times the payment was often described as a "gift."

Advocates were always easy prey for satirists, who charged them with lack of scruples and conscience, as well as with greed. During the course of the fourth century

A.D., corruption, bribery, ignorance, and incompetence in the profession reached its height. One observer lamented: "We see the most violent and rapacious classes of men besieging the houses of the rich, cunningly creating lawsuits."

Advocates were not, however, the only members of the Roman legal profession. A step beneath them were the *consulting lawyers* who issued legal advice for a fee, but would not or could not plead cases in court on their clients' behalf. In a class by themselves were the *jurisconsults*, a group of legal specialists who came to dominate the profession in Rome. Like many of the earliest legal professionals, these experts had once been drawn from the priesthood. They began as a distinct class of religious officials who reached their status as legal specialists only after years of service in government, which included judicial service. Some of them devoted themselves in later life exclusively to the specialized study of the law. These were the earliest jurisconsults, all of whom were aristocrats

Courtrooms were often the scenes of great personal dramas and confrontations. (Advertising woodcut for Jeanie Deans; or, The Heart of Midlothian, *1860)*

working for honor, power, and influence, not for pay. It was they who advised all parties in the Roman government—lawmakers, judges, advocates, and clients—on matters of law. In the process, they did much to help shape the Roman legal system.

Although advocates were the celebrities of the legal system, the jurisconsults were from the most prominent families of Rome and had reached their positions only after distinguished careers in government, so they had the higher status. By the end of the third century B.C., they had begun to hold public consultations at which they gave their opinions on points of law to those who would learn, although giving formal instruction was regarded as beneath their dignity.

A typical jurisconsult came from the select circle of families who supplied the high officials of Rome. After completing his basic schooling, a young man aspiring to the profession would enter the household of an eminent jurisconsult, often one known to the young man's own family. The aspirant learned by following and observing the jurisconsult in all his varied activities, taking notes, reading on his own, and asking questions of his mentor. The education thus achieved was primarily practical, and indeed throughout most of Roman history, theoretical and academic study had little place, unlike earlier Greece and later medieval Europe.

By the first century B.C., jurisconsults were being drawn from a wider range of social classes; not all of them were aristocrats. Those of less exalted origins certainly began to expect and receive pay for their services. As public sparring increased between jurisconsults debating points of law, formal schools were first established. The two main schools were founded by Labeo and Capito, two legal rivals, in the early centuries of the empire. These schools had no permanent quarters. Lectures were given in the master's home if it was large enough, or a public room was rented for that purpose. The schools developed a small permanent staff of teachers and writers, rather than practicing consultants. These teachers had little status, as evidenced by the fact that they were paid by fee, but had no rights to recover their fees by legal action.

Throughout their history, jurisconsults were purely advisors; they always looked down upon advocates and themselves entered the judicial fray only in very rare cases, on behalf of close friends or high nobility or on an important and extremely controversial point of law. Their disdain for appearing in court may partly reflect the fact that their lectures on points of law fared poorly in court against the emotional speeches of the advocates. In any case, they regarded themselves not as partisans but as impartial interpreters and guardians of the law, advising all parties. Indeed, clients and their advocates would often consult several jurisconsults, taking the opinion that best suited their needs.

For practical legal support, clients turned not only to courtroom advocates and orators but also to a lesser group of *procurators*, who specialized in drawing up fairly extensive legal documents and contracts as the Roman judicial and trial systems became more complex. The *tabelliones* were lesser draftsmen who produced much simpler articles on request. In the major cities, such as Rome, lesser functionaries also operated. *Secretaries* and *scribes* attached to the church or to the judicial staff developed considerable legal skill, which they put to use writing legal documents for private clients as a source of extra income. Sycophants also operated in Rome, for in the early period, as in Greece, no state prosecutors existed; while their reputation continued to be bad, they did not have the destructive power in Rome that they had had in Greece.

If the jurisconsults of the Roman Republic created and shaped Roman law, those of the later Roman Empire developed and elaborated on it. It was the painstaking care that the Romans took in codifying the law and training legal experts to apply it that led to the high state of political cohesion and effectiveness that was the crowning feature of the Roman Empire. But with the growth of the empire came an expansion of government bureaucracy, a rapid growth in the number of government offices and officials needed to deal with the enormous demands of public administration. Instead of being independent aristocrats, later generations of jurisconsults were drawn from rising families whose members became legal specialists when young and spent their lives as salaried employees of the government.

Under the emperor Augustus the drafting of laws was taken out of the hands of jurisconsults, made routine, and given to lesser lawyers and scribes. Jurisconsults were attached to each magistrate to give legal advice, but to still differences of opinion, Augustus began the practice of calling only a few leading jurisconsults to serve on a higher advisory body called the *consilium principis*. As a result, the opinions of lower or unauthorized jurisconsults came to be little heeded. Gradually the opinions of individual jurisconsults came to be disregarded altogether, since the decision reached by a consilium was expressed anonymously, as if unanimous, with no dissent or variance of opinion recorded.

As the *consilium principis* drew from an ever-smaller and more elite group of jurists, the *responsa prudentium* (legal opinion) of the group became increasingly predictable. The Valentinian Law of Citations of 426 A.D. made such opinions the basis of the Roman legal code. The object of establishing a formal written code was to eliminate as much as possible potential for dissent and differing interpretations. Finally, in 534 A.D., Justinian took this process to its logical conclusion when he gathered up what he considered the best writings and opinions on Roman law into a single code, which was—in his ideal—to be the supreme legal guide for the empire. Regarding any further changes as unnecessary and any differences of opinion as divisive, he banned further interpretation of the legal code by jurisconsults and ordered the burning of all existing jurisconsults' opinions that had not been included in the code. He was not fully successful in either endeavor, but his actions helped set the tone of medieval legal activities, in which the written code was predominant. In later Rome, most of the best legal talent went either into the imperial bureaucracy or into the rising Christian church where, after the fall of the Western Roman Empire, medieval law took shape.

While legal experts lost much of their power in the late Western Roman Empire, in the Eastern Roman Empire, centered in Byzantium (Constantinople), legal practitioners were still important, becoming even more so in the late fifth and early sixth centuries. There, bureaucratic jurisconsults were still important interpreters and shapers of the law, and advocates were active and highly regarded. While in the West advocates were still primarily orators, in the Eastern Empire it became the custom for advocates to attend law school, notably the one at Berytus (now Beirut) for four or five years. Those who had merely attended rhetoric schools, where law was taught as a sideline, came to be laughed out of court by the magistrates or shown the door "like very criminals," as one contemporary put it. By 460 A.D., legal study was required for advocates, who had to pass an examination and show a certificate of legal knowledge from a professor before practicing the art. Combining both legal knowledge and practical skill, these advocates were rewarded with many high offices in the Byzantine (Eastern Roman) Empire.

Roman law had taken an extraordinary step in the history of the legal profession. It had made the first solid, large-scale attempt to give society a codified set of rules by which to live—rules that would guide all people in their interactions with one another, and would give officials a point of reference in detecting transgression of the law and in deciding appropriate punishment or settlement.

At the other end of Eurasia, China soon made the same attempt. Chinese jurists devised a written and formalized code of law in 653 A.D., during the early years of the T'ang dynasty. Oriental law bore little similarity to Roman and later Germanic developments in the field, however. Chinese law generally placed far greater importance on the individual's obligations to society than on society's responsibility to protect the rights of the individual. Moreover, the Chinese legal tradition was deeply rooted in the Confucian idea that order derives from proper education rather than punishment. Punishment was called for only in extreme and rare cases. It was only during brief intervals of Chinese history that the ideals of *Legalism*—which called for strict punishment and reward systems—were popularized over the more liberal principles of *Confucianism.*

The Legalist view dominated Chinese law under the strict rule of the short-lived and tyrannical Ch'in dynasty, 221-206 B.C. So severe and hated was the law put forth then that, from the end of the Ch'in dynasty until the 20th century, legal procedures barely existed at all as a feature of Chinese law, and few cases were tried in the courts. When they were, their results were practically predetermined, and defendants were not even permitted the representation of lawyers or advocates. The belief was

Lawyers like this nattily mustachioed advocate often cut a dashing figure in the courtroom. (From Source Book of French Advertising Art, *Faber & Faber, 1970)*

that if defendants were innocent, they ought to be able to prove it by their honest statements rather than through the polished maneuvers of professional spokesmen. The legal profession in China, from ancient times to the very recent past, was left to a few crafty speechwriters and counselors, who helped prepare their clients to defend themselves.

For many centuries following the disintegration of the Roman Empire, the legal profession in the Western world fared little better than it did in China and elsewhere in the East. Europe's feudal system of social organization placed great stress on obligation, and little on rights. Moreover, justice was administered in local courts that made little use of formal trials and had no need for third-party legal representatives. The law itself was so informal and self-serving for the elite ruling class that legal counselors had few codes or precedents to refer to—and few magistrates cared to be informed of them where they did exist.

A legal profession based on the Roman model did survive in some form within the Catholic church, where experts continued to interpret church or *canon* law. The church was one of the few surviving institutions of the Roman Empire, and its canon law was a code of rules and procedures in the Roman tradition. The tradition was carried on by *priests* and *clerics* rather than professional lawyers as such. Still, a vital intellectual movement persisted in formulating and interpreting canon law, and the *ecclesiastical* (church) courts kept alive the Roman tradition of legal procedure until that tradition could be restored to the civil and criminal courts of the state. If anything, the keen involvement of the Catholic priesthood in church law lent an air of respectability to the pursuit of the legal career in the secular world.

Legal analysis and procedure made great strides in the Arab world, after the Prophet Mohammad founded the Moslem or Islamic religion in the seventh century. In Islamic law, the religious courts of the judges known as *qadis* were the most influential, but they rarely admitted legal representatives, as both prosecutors and defendants were generally required to plead their own cases. Legal counsel was sought privately, and at times the *qadi* himself sought the advice of a professional jurist, or *mufti*.

In the Islamic world, law—religious, civil, criminal, and even commercial—was reviewed in terms of morality. Interpretation was based on the teachings of the Prophet Mohammad, taking into account orthodox viewpoints, the public interest, and the consensus (*ijma*) of authoritative Islamic jurists. Clearly, whatever legal specialists existed within this system were concerned primarily with religious speculation—though it was speculation that had very real effects on the everyday lives of individuals whose cases passed through the courts. The pattern prevails today in much of the Arab world.

When Europe began to experience a renaissance of interest in Classical learning in the 12th century, law once again surfaced as a significant feature of Western civilization. —nterest revived in studying and applying the principles and procedures of Roman law. Its influence had never completely died, but the feudal structure of society had not generally required any centralized legal authority or formal legal code—nor any professional class of legal representatives, counselors, or scholars. These things survived thanks mostly to the church's maintainance of the traditional forms and processes of Roman law. In some parts of France and Italy, however, where fairly considerable regions had to be administered by somewhat centralized governments, the institution of Roman law, and the subsequent need for professional lawyers, never really ceased at all. Still, we consider the Renaissance period to have cradled the rebirth of a widespread interest in the application of Roman law.

The most obvious reason for this rekindled interest was the general rediscovery of Classical culture—its arts, letters, and institutions. But perhaps the immediate reason was more practical than scholarly. The age of feudalism was drawing its last breaths, and rulers were administering and controlling larger and more cosmopolitan areas—whole states rather than simple manors. This called for more centralized, complex, and better organized forms of law—and a special class of people who could understand, formulate, and interpret them. Nowhere in history was there a more fitting example to guide the new rulers of Europe than in the ancient Roman legal texts. Considering the authoritative position of the church (many of the leaders of state were themselves priests), and its long-time endorsement of Roman law, it is little wonder that the new governments turned to that same source of inspiration.

With complex political relationships replacing the simple lord-vassal ones and with an increasingly complex economic order overcoming the older agricultural manorial societies, there was good reason for new interest in Roman law and the legal profession. All this happened very slowly, however. Although cities were growing and feudalism was waning by the 12th century, it took a considerable time before law or court systems were truly centralized. Most cities created their own laws, along with courts to try mostly petty crimes. These courts were regarded as the "low justice" of the land. The church, royal, and military courts to which serious crimes and lawsuits were brought constituted the "high justice."

Professional lawyers soon became active at both levels, but particularly in the high courts. In England, where a great centralizing effort had taken place after the Norman Conquest of the 11th century A.D., *procurators* (who had important roles in preparing and reviewing legal documents) and *advocates* became established practitioners in both church and military courts. The centralized *common law* of England fell into the hands of an elite group of advocates who represented clients in the royal courts. This group received special legal training at the famous Inns of Court in London, and the best of them attained the lofty status of *serjeant*. Those in apprenticeship were known as *barristers*.

The revival of Classical culture had a profound effect on the legal profession in more ways than one. There was a scholarly interest in Roman procedures and legal codes, particularly the Justinian *Digest*, which became a standard text in most medieval universities where law was taught. This scholarly approach was brought to maturity by a dignified group of jurists known as the *glossators*, who practiced in northern Italy during the 12th century, and the *postglossators*, who practiced in both Italy and France during the 13th and 14th centuries. While their interest in Roman law was intense, however, they were not practicing advocates or attorneys. They were concerned instead with the theological and academic ramifications of the law. Most law departments taught only canon law, and then primarily as an exercise in logic rather than as training for a practical and active career. Both Roman and Germanic law were treated in light of the Scriptures. Nevertheless, any serious interest in the study of law strengthened the profession.

Another development played an even more important role in the rise of the legal profession. That development was the revival of commerce, which carried Western culture from the Renaissance into the early modern age. It was the rush of commerce and trade, sailing and carting, fairs and markets—in short, of business—that demanded a greater complexity of legal statutes, and a more appropriately trained corps of professionals to write and interpret them. As European businesses began to make transactions with paper money and credit rather than with gold and silver, as professional *haulers* incurred greater and less direct liabilities—in other words, as business transactions became increasingly elaborate—law and lawsuits also increased in complexity. The rise of *mercantile* and *commercial law* opened up a vast new range of lucrative lawsuits for pioneer lawyers to handle. As these new practitioners enthusiastically went about their business, they acquired a reputation for using tactics that many people found questionable. This shady image quickly spread to all lawyers, who were both honored for their power and knowledge—and hated for their sometimes devious and selfish cunning. One lawyer

Whether in official courtroom or ad hoc judicial chambers, attorneys were expected to make eloquent pleas for their clients. (From London Illustrated News)

of the times made no apologies. "I am a good lawyer," he stated flatly. "Often I've made right out of wrong and wrong out of right, as it suited me."

Many new opportunities had begun to open up for lawyers. Besides the advocates and procurators, *notaries* had become significant specialists in authenticating legal documents, and in arranging and drafting them as well. *Legal secretaries* and *clerks* attached themselves to noteworthy officials, jurists, and teachers in hopes of bettering themselves. In the universities, meanwhile, the *doctors of the law*, who taught canon law, attained a high status. While the scholars brought about a greater understanding of Roman legal traditions and local Germanic customs, it was the commercial and *civil lawyers*, acting as advocates in court and counselors in private matters, who became the shapers of the law, forging it into a distinctly modern tool by which a rapidly changing commercial and cosmopolitan society might be sustained and enhanced.

Even so, the law remained for many years in the hands of a few local and ecclesiastical authorities. It is little wonder that lawyers found it so difficult to practice when counts, dukes, burghers, even kings and bishops all scrambled to hold "court privileges" over as vast a territory as possible. In doing so, they fought for the exclusive privilege not only of trying cases, but—more important—of collecting the fines levied.

So hotly contested was the fight for court privileges that no less a document than the English Magna Carta supported the court privileges of local barons against the encroaching claims of the king. English town charters frequently granted these privileges to local counts, who might pocket up to two-thirds of the fines taken in and receive a yearly cash stipend from the town as well. Bishops fought to retain their lucrative privileges against the provosts and burghers of newly formed towns. Ecclesiastical, township, royal, and estate jurisdictions frequently overlapped and caused serious bickering among those attempting to cash in on their "rightful" court privileges. In the midst of all this, there was clearly little room for intruding lawyers. Cases were often tried and decided by a single magistrate or circuit judge. Defendants pleaded their own cases and—it was commonly assumed—would have their innocence displayed by the mercy of God, if innocent they were. Logic and legalisms had little to do with justice, just as civil law was in no way distinct from canon law.

As lawyers gained importance in the 16th and 17th centuries, however, *court trials* and *juries* became more central to Western justice. In this period, witnesses and defendants came to rely more heavily on the courtroom representation and private counsel of trained lawyers acting as procurators, advocates, and notaries. Governments increasingly took over the administration of justice, making the payment of fines less immediately rewarding to the elite class of aristocrats and church officials controlling the courts. Legal decisions thereby became more impartial, and magistrates and juries were more likely to hear *counter-evidence* and *cross-examinations* on both sides of an issue. The very presence of the legal profession helped promote the idea of justice for all, at least as an ideal in Western civilization. *Courts of appeal* represented a still further advance in this direction, giving disgruntled losers of legal battles a chance to have their cases heard by higher courts. All of these developments contributed to making the lawyer a central figure in the courtroom.

The eventual separation of civil law from canon law and the continued growth of commerce and industry also contributed to the rise of lawyers. In the university, the teachers and scholars of the law began to take a more practical approach than they had previously, giving more emphasis to the arts of advocacy and legal writing. Their influence on the profession varied significantly with the times and circumstances, but in general they responded with some skill and vigor to the need for a more practical orientation in the field.

While lawyers once had been forbidden entrance to the manorial courts (the *hallmotes*), their presence in court gradually came to be considered a right of citizenship, a process virtually completed by the 18th century. Other changes came to the legal profession over the centuries. The quality of available lawyers in the early Industrial Age was much higher than in medieval times. Medieval lawyers were often little more than sworn-in townsmen or farmers, with no education and no more than common knowledge of what the law was. But 18th-century lawyers were almost always well-bred men of distinction, with a great deal of training, a fine educational background, and considerable usefulness in society. From the 1500's to the 1700's they came to take on more and more importance as their status and repute heightened accordingly.

The English serjeants of the Elizabethan era were among the grandest of courtiers, and the royal judges were chosen strictly from among them. The Inns of Court, where legal experts were trained, became increasingly snobbish; in the 17th century its membership excluded from their rolls *attorneys* and *solicitors*, who had first arisen as special agents in lawsuits the century before. Advocates and barristers alone remained as the representatives of this haughty institution; even the serjeants were eventually dissolved, leaving the barristers as an elite group of lawyers dominating the British higher courts. From the 18th century on, barristers were not even directly engaged by clients; even today English barristers work with clients only through *attorneys* or *solicitors*—as all lawyers who are not barristers have been known for the past century.

Other groups of lawyers enjoyed a rather lofty status, too, although few were as powerful as the English barristers. Reminiscent of the organizations of the Roman jurisconsults was the aristocratic French Order of Advocates (*Ordre des Avocats*), which permitted its practicing members to receive only gifts for their efforts rather than wages. Even notaries have been highly esteemed on the European continent. And the French and Dutch jurists and Italian doctors of law were always greatly revered for their keen insight and wisdom in the field.

The English system of dividing the legal profession into groups with very different levels of status and responsibility is not typical of other European countries. On the Continent, advocates represent their clients in court, as the English barristers do—and procurators draw up legal documents and handle the more technical aspects of litigation as the English solicitors do; but advocates and procurators are not nearly so distinguishable as barristers and solicitors in terms of training, responsibility, professional stature, or financial compensation. The American legal profession began with the English model, but ultimately went its own way.

Throughout their modern history, lawyers have held rather prominent positions in society. As far back as the Renaissance, lawyers from some 27 families dominated Venice's legislature, accounting for over half of its councillors. Lawyers were quick to acquire political prominence, not particularly because of their legal education (many early lawyers were rather poor students), but more because of their aristocratic origins. Their professional training only added skill and knowledge to their already-existing claims to social and political power. Lawyers of the early modern era were often regarded as haughty craftsmen, skillful in the art of deception and always on guard to support the *status quo* (existing state).

As a group, these early lawyers were often unimaginative, professionally uncreative, and politically reactionary. Most focused on the "letter of the law," with little regard for its usefulness, timeliness, or intent. These lawyers were too preoccupied with stating the law and applying it appropriately to give any heed to sophisticated legal analyses or interpretations. They were not employed to make, shape, alter, or interpret laws, but merely to recall them. Whether in England or in continental Europe, they acted as if there was one correct and appropriate set of statutes perfectly designed to offer complete justice to an entire society. If such statutes were found to fall short of directing action on a given case, advocates or solicitors might recall the principle of *stare decisis*, indicating that similar cases should be decided similarly. This principle allowed lawyers freedom of interpretation on only the most limited of terms. They might recall cases similar to the one they were representing or reviewing, in order to apply whatever guidance might be available in earlier court decisions, relevant statutes, or even social customs. But while lawyers often looked back in time for guidance, they seldom looked forward to offer new interpretations and ideas for the future. The greatest initiative in shaking the legal profession from this backward-looking position came from the new nation of the United States.

The early Colonial lawyers drew heavily from the Elizabethan tradition of their homeland. They were especially well-known for their long, elaborate courtroom speeches. This did not endear them to the Puritans, who called them masters of the "babblative art." Many Puritans wanted to do away with lawyers altogether, thinking it best that "every ploughman" plead his own case. They considered it somehow not moral for one person to speak on behalf of another, especially when God's will was supposed to be displayed through the direct actions, reactions, and testimonies of witnesses and defendants themselves. As a result, the legal profession in North America for a long time lagged behind that of England. In part this was due to the primitive economy of the Colonies and their dependence on England. By contrast, in England, once the Commercial Revolution began, barristers and solicitors rapidly ascended to positions of social and political prominence, for their skills were vital to the smooth working of the rapidly growing economy.

Early American lawyers can hardly be said to have been "trained" at all; very few were even minimally educated. Even as late as the end of the 17th century, New York had only seven lawyers; two were ex-convicts from abroad, one was a former *dance master*, and one had been a *glover*. Those American lawyers who did receive training usually had an education combining a study of the Greek and Latin classics, along with practical oratory. Most were merchants, like Samuel Sewall, or planters, like William Fitzhugh, who used the very practical understanding of commercial law gained through their own business experience to help others. It was people such as these who really formed the nucleus of the American legal profession and eventually made it an integral part of American commercial and business life, well before criminal or civil lawyers came into public prominence.

Commercial lawyers were the first to gain acceptance in America, but no lawyers enjoyed great esteem before the Revolutionary War. In 1658, the colony of Virginia actually banished all lawyers from its territory; they apparently agreed with New Englander John Hull who complained that their practice of law was "very much like a lottery—great charge, little benefit." The Carolina constitution condemned the profession too, claiming it to be a "base and vile thing to plead for money or reward." Throughout the Colonies, lawyers were seen as being devious, overly expensive, and socially worthless—even corrupting.

Part of the reason for so negative an attitude toward American lawyers was that they did not have the aristocratic base that their English counterparts did. The laws of inheritance that so occupied British lawyers had little or no relevance to American society, so no landed gentry demanded legal services. There was too much land in America for laws of inheritance to be of much importance. Moreover, there was hardly any "common law" existing at any level in the politically and culturally segregated colonies. As late as the end of the 18th century, Thomas Jefferson was still referring to Massachusetts law as "foreign law." Colonial laws were so

Throughout history, some lawyers have specialized as consultants, rather than as courtroom advocates. (From Frank Leslie's Popular Monthly Magazine)

local, piecemeal, incoherent, and ambiguous that they were easily manipulated by sly lawyers seeking profit and prestige.

In Britain, barristers could proudly boast of their aristocratic heritage and their training at the prestigious Inns of Court. The British legal system was made up of specialists: Barristers represented clients only in the royal courts. Attorneys specialized in drawing up documents such as wills and deeds. Notaries specialized in authenticating legal documents. But America had no Inns of Court to give lawyers either prestige or proper training. Nor were there specializations or rankings within the profession to allow significant refinement or progress in any particular area.

Jeremiah Gridley was keenly aware of these problems when he warned John Adams that "the difficulties of the profession are much greater here than in England." As he explained: "A lawyer in this country must study common law, civil law, natural law, and admiralty law; and must do the duty of a counsellor, a lawyer, an attorney, a solicitor, and even a scrivener." As a matter of fact, many *clerks* and *scriveners* (those who made handwritten copies of documents) did a considerable amount of legal work as part of their general clerical duties, and it was not uncommon for them to climb the professional ladder and become lawyers themselves. There was plenty of opportunity in the legal profession for industrious, self-educated climbers.

American lawyers had little competition from the prestigious British lawyers, who were eagerly sought but rarely attracted by the Colonies. The greatest difficulty for Americans trying to forge successful legal careers was in obtaining suitable formal training. Such training virtually did not exist until Blackstone's *Commentaries on the Laws of England* became standardized text material during the Revolutionary War era. Before that, Sir Edward Coke's legal treatises had been the chief educational resource, but offered little of the rich practical and theoretical base provided by Blackstone. At about the same time, it was becoming increasingly common for American lawyers to have graduated from universities such as Harvard and Yale. Fortunately, the training of American lawyers improved at precisely the same time that the British governors of the Colonies were relying more and more heavily on the services of English lawyers to help maintain the King's law over increasingly obstinate subjects. During this period, American lawyers truly rose to the challenge in their assessment and legal interpretation of the tensions between the Colonies and mother England.

Most American lawyers had a wealth of practical experience, since it was that which had traditionally provided their training grounds. They became particularly adept at trying maritime disputes, since overseas trade and smuggling were a prime focus of tension with the British. They quickly learned all phases of *maritime law*, including the flourishing new specialties of *contract* and *insurance law*. Early on, British governors had thought little of appointing American lawyers to posts in the vice-admiralty courts that maintained jurisdiction over maritime disputes. As tensions increased, however, they turned more and more to their homeland for staff, citing a preference for the better-educated barristers from the Inns of Court. Meanwhile, as the American legal profession matured, Colonial laws became increasingly "common" and less local. The standardization of legal training based on Blackstone's *Commentaries* aided this process, as did the generally higher quality of Colonial lawyers graduating from prestigious universities—in a rising number of cases, from the Inns of Court itself.

The British soon began to be intimidated by the growth of "American Law," along with its own brand of common law courts and distinctly American lawyers. In response, the British not only removed American lawyers from the vice-admiralty courts—the only formally recognized British jurisdictional stronghold in the Colonies—they also took bold steps to expand the authority of those courts. The British referred as many cases as they reasonably could to the vice-admiralty courts, particularly those with dangerous political overtones. In that way, they kept American lawyers at a distance from the process of interpreting British law. In response to this state of affairs, American lawyers developed a legal philosophy that had the immediate effect of legitimizing and even popularizing the ensuing rebellion, and the long-range effect of democratizing the legal profession and the law itself. From that point on, American lawyers became the pacesetters in modernizing the legal profession to its present-day standards.

The new legal philosophy that culminated in the American institution of democracy had actually been rooted in the new nation's European heritage. English lawyers first obtained professional rights from the king with the signing of the Magna Carta. In the 17th century, two prominent British lawyers—Sir Edward Coke and John Seldon—were instrumental in devising the *Petition of Right*. This document granted lawyers the right to question even a monarch on points of law and legislation, and also gave any citizen the right to defend himself at a fair trial. The first right, concerning freedom of speech, allowed lawyers to question the wisdom of a law. The second protected citizens against secret and unwarranted imprisonment. American lawyers continued this struggle for personal and civil liberties both for themselves as professionals and for the citizenry in general. In one of the most noteworthy landmarks along this path, a bold young lawyer from Pennsylvania, Andrew Hamilton, fought a brilliant battle on behalf of journalist John Peter Zenger. The immediate issue was Zenger's freedom to print a newspaper article that criticized a New York governor. The case was won by Hamilton and Zenger, establishing a precedent for freedom of the press. This is but one example of how lawyers were instrumental in the establishment of basic rights of citizenship and, eventually, the American democratic system.

The ideas that inspired the American Revolution had been brewing for some time. The 17th-century English philosopher John Locke (1632-1704) had stirred controversy with his insistence that kings or other civil authorities had no inherent right to govern as they wished, but, rather, an obligation to rule in the best interest of the governed. The 18th-century French philosopher Jean Jacques Rousseau similarly noted that governments had a right to rule only insofar as they upheld their part of the "social contract"—in other words, only as long as they ruled with respect for the public welfare. Other political theorists, philosophers, and legal scholars joined this great debate, which found full expression in the American and French revolutions of the late 18th century.

The principle established by those revolutions was that monarchs had no "divine right" to impose their leadership on others, that the only true law in the universe was the "natural law" by which the governed clearly inherited basic rights and freedoms. The writers of the American Declaration of Independence called this the right of "life, liberty, and the pursuit of happiness." Attached to the Constitution of the new United States was a basic Bill of Rights, including freedom of speech, freedom of religion, and other "rights" that had rarely been granted by prior governments or rulers. The French, too, called for similar rights for the citizenry, along with the establishment of democracy, but their attempts eventually failed. It was the American experience that would considerably alter the scope of the legal profession.

The Revolutionary era was one of great progress for American lawyers. In the years leading up to the war, lawyers were on the front lines in the attack on British rule. They cited the arguments for "natural law" and the "natural rights" of citizenship. They waged legal battles against improper representation and for freedom of speech, commerce, and the bearing of arms. In the two decades before the war, they rose, as a profession, from second-class status to roles of leadership within society. When the Declaration of Independence was finally drafted, nearly half of its 56 signers were lawyers. And in the delicate, early years of the Republic, the careful shap-

ing of a new, powerful nation was left largely in the hands of the legal profession.

For all of this success, American lawyers were slow in establishing adequate training requirements and standards. In general, training had improved. A great many practicing lawyers at the end of the century had college or university educations, and between 1750 and 1775 some 150 of them had even attended the Inns of Court in London. But it was not until 1779 that William and Mary became the first college to establish—after endless prodding by none less than Thomas Jefferson—a separate department of law. Five years later, the Litchfield Law School was founded by a judge, but it was only a private training institute, as were those that followed its lead. Finally, in 1817, the Harvard Law School became the first university-affiliated law school. One of its professors—Justice Joseph Story—was to have a profound effect on altering the basis of legal training from the old European system of apprenticeship to the dis-

Lawyers in Europe's common law countries often have higher status than judges, who are primarily civil servants. (By Honoré Daumier, authors' archives)

tinctly American method of formal professional studies following a liberal arts education. To this day, the American legal profession stands alone in its emphasis on the formal training and liberal education of its recruits rather than on the more common apprenticeship method.

Despite the progress made toward better and more formal legal education, even by 1860 none of the 21 law schools in the country had any entrance requirements, and only a few provided adequate training. The most common route into the profession was still via apprenticeship. Young *clerks*, *accountants*, or *legal assistants* who gained the confidence and patronage of an acting lawyer in good standing could get enough training to become lawyers themselves.

In terms of formal recognition, prospective lawyers could simply petition the courts to swear them before the bar, and they were thereby officially penned into the list of current practitioners. That step was fairly easy, if they had the backing of a reputable lawyer. From that point on, they embarked on their apprenticeship. This consisted of following the mentor everywhere and keeping their ears and eyes open. They would learn how clients were handled, the techniques and procedures of courtroom advocacy, and—hopefully—something of the ethical standards binding lawyers to an adamant upholding not only of the clients' rights but also of the spirit and the letter of the law. The most formal portion of their training was the diligent study of Blackstone's *Commentaries* and perhaps some other less imposing texts.

Gradually, novice lawyers, clerks, or legal assistants would begin to handle more and more of their mentor's responsibilities. The first task they were likely to be assigned would be the preparation of legal proceedings by way of drafting suitable legal documents and writing up contracts. These would then be used by the senior lawyer in court or private counsel in fulfilling the total obligation to the client. The novice might later take on an entire case alone, and finally, assume a substantial share of the caseload of the practice. At this point, the young lawyer might become a partner to the teacher, or else set up an independent practice. The success or failure of the lawyer's career depended ultimately on the quality of his apprenticeship training and service.

The same career path was followed, more or less, throughout the Western world, although the responsibilities of lawyers differed. American lawyers continued to handle virtually every aspect of a case on their own, while in Europe, responsibility remained strictly divided between those authorized to prepare legal documents, those who officially approved them, those who offered private counsel, and those who represented clients in court. But on both continents, the status of the profession improved steadily. By the middle of the 19th century, a substantial percentage of the membership of Parliament was represented by barristers, while in the United States lawyers dominated Congress. Lawyers also dominated the national legislatures of France, Germany, Italy, and most other countries of the newly industrialized world.

A major breakthrough in the education of American lawyers came after the development in 1871 of the *case method* of training. Proposed by Christopher Columbus Langdell, the dean of the Harvard Law School, it focused on studies of actual court cases and judicial reviews and decisions. The long-range effects of this exciting new way of offering formal education to legal trainees was to make American law schools the most prominent in the world, and eventually to make the American legal profession the least dependent on apprenticeship of any other comparable system. Thereafter, professional standards became increasingly rigid, with college degrees becoming ever more necessary to practice. Ultimately, standardized state bar examinations capped postgraduate study in an approved law school and preceded admittance to the bar. The legal profession became more elite and influential than ever, and professional associations were formed to standardize professional codes of ethics and to further enhance communication among active practitioners.

On the frontier, a lawyer needed only a pen, some paper, a box, and a carpetbag to set up business, as here in what is probably the Oklahoma land rush of 1889. (Library of Congress)

Although the first bar association in America was formed as early as 1802 in Philadelphia, the first truly influential one was the Association of the Bar of the City of New York, established in 1870. The national American Bar Association came into existence in 1878.

As the Western world became increasingly industrialized, a cosmopolitan form of society rapidly replaced the rural, highly localized one that had dominated since the earliest epochs of history. Complex relationships replaced previously simple ones between all classes of groups and individuals: buyers and sellers, manufacturers and distributors, laborers and management. Laws became increasingly complex, in turn, and the consequent demand for better laws and lawyers became inevitable. Both were needed for situations that previously had laid little claim to judicial review or state action. Most of the Western governments—led by Britain and America—were becoming more democratic than anyone had imagined possible (or tolerable) a century earlier. Workers' rights, children's rights, consumers' rights—all demanded state legislation and the response of the legal profession. Lawsuits became more complex and commonplace; criminal law had largely become separate from civil law, and all government law became increasingly separate from canon law and religious standards.

The 19th century saw rapid growth of the practicing bar in Great Britain. From less than 2,500 in 1830, its membership almost tripled by 1880. Barristers—who had for some time been thought of as little more than genteel windbags—gained considerable recognition and professional esteem. Their reliance on the lower bar—the solicitors and attorneys, who alone could employ barristers on behalf of their own clients—kept them ever mindful of the need to maintain cordial relations, both socially and politically, with their "inferiors." They were, however, still above the common ordeal of seeking business directly from clients and requesting fees from them.

City attorneys were an exclusive lot, often dining in their own private, elegantly appointed club. (From Harper's Weekly, *November 26, 1887)*

Barristers were much more strictly supervised than American lawyers, having to answer to the Inns of Court concerning their professional behavior and moral conduct. This responsibility added to their air of distinction as a group.

The British had traditionally placed little emphasis on formal education in legal training. Still, in 1872, a standard examination finally became a requirement for admission to the British bar. Barristers were actually the last among the British professions to take steps toward formal standards, and even then they were stumbling ones. The barristers' test was ridiculed by practitioners, professors, and novices alike as being so simple that virtually no legal knowledge was necessary to pass it. The real problem continued to be the profession's strong stand against specific educational requirements or training. As one bitter observer put it: "The paramount evil of the ordeal of examination is that it discourages what I may call the principles of apprenticeship. The three years'

A classic comic character was part-time farmer, part-time lawyer Solon Shingle. (Advertising woodcut for The People's Lawyer, *Boston, 1839)*

preparation for the Bar ought to be spent in the chambers of counsel."

The standing of the British bar had a considerable effect on the development of the legal profession throughout the world during the late 19th century as well as the 20th century. Britain's leadership in industrial strength and commercial prowess was rivaled only by that of the United States. Moreover, for much of this period the British continued to rule colonies all over the world. Many a legal professional banned from practicing at home for one reason or another could set up practice in one of the colonies. It was assumed that only second-rate barristers, solicitors, and attorneys took up practice in distant colonies such as India, Australia, Hong Kong, and the West Indies. But in truth the profession was overcrowded within England by the last quarter of the 19th century. Many young lawyers headed for the colonies simply for the sake of finding opportunity where little existed at home. A good number of these proved to be highly competent and helped to set a strong precedent throughout the world in the organization of the legal profession along British lines.

As the West embarked on the modern industrial era, the concept and application of the law underwent considerable changes that had profound effects on the maturing legal profession. When strong, centralized nation-states had first begun to emerge from medieval feudalism, Roman law had been reduced from a general system of justice to the notion of *quod principi placuit habet vigorem*: "the prince's pleasure is law." Lawyers were bound, then, to restrict their services essentially to those elite groups whose pleasure it was to dictate and modify (when convenient) the law. They were frequently patronized by aristocrats and bishops, and by their services supported legal systems based on feudal birthrights and privileged status.

During the 18th and 19th centuries, however, as industrialization altered the whole structure of society, *negotiated rights* came more and more into play, as birthrights became less and less significant. For professional lawyers, this change meant a much greater emphasis on rights, privileges, and obligations established by *contract*, rather than by status. Lawyers had to learn much more about the preparation and interpretation of contracts, and less about simple oratory. Increasingly, they received fees from common clients—laborers, merchants, and householders—rather than receiving patronage and favors from satisfied aristocrats and gentry.

When these changes first began to occur, it was feared that the acceptance of fees and the willingness to represent anyone who could afford them—regardless of the client's social position—would hurt the public esteem of the legal profession as a whole. Gradually, however, lawyers saw that there was more opportunity in private practice and government or business service than in catering to an elite aristocracy that was dwindling in numbers as well as in influence. This became particularly clear as *criminal law* and *litigation* emerged as specialties from the general field of civil law. Previously, lawyers had spent much of their time preparing legal documents, such as contracts and agreements. Litigation—the initiation of legal actions in the courts—had rarely been taken seriously, and in some places, such as in colonial America, amounted to little more than a popular form of entertainment. But from this period on, an increasing number of lawyers would be specializing in litigation. Criminal law, too, remained largely overlooked until Cesare Beccaria published his *Crimes and Punishments* in 1764, sharply criticizing governments for not codifying criminal law. He protested the fact that criminal codes had been left to the whims and self-interest of absolutist authorities.

Both litigation and criminal procedure were greatly enhanced by movements to strictly codify laws. Picking up on the tradition established by 17th- and 18th-century French, Scandinavian, and Dutch jurists, the German *Pandectists* worked hard at establishing a codified system of laws. Previously, the greatest effort on this front had

been that of Napoleon, who established his famous *Napoleonic Codes* between 1804 and 1810. The German effort culminated in the great civil code of 1900, which inspired later similar developments in China, Japan, Italy, Switzerland, and elsewhere. The idea of establishing rigid national legal codes had its greatest support on the European continent. In England, the United States, and Canada, there was a far greater reliance on the gradual evolution of law through judicial decisions and custom than on a blanket system of justice imposed by whatever authorities happened to be in power at a given time.

In England, Jeremy Bentham and others fought hard to create a standard legal code that would be comprehensible to lay people. Judges and lawyers fought just as hard to suppress any "code-law system," favoring instead the case-law system developed through the everyday activities, presentations, and interpretations of judges and lawyers. Case law, they argued, was more sensitive to individual cases and circumstances, as well as

In fiction, at least, lawyers like this public prosecutor try to dupe criminals into confessing their misdeeds. (Advertising woodcut from Clairvoyance; or, The Man With the Wax Figures, *Brooklyn, 1867)*

to subtle changes in society, while not abandoning consistency, integrity, or the wisdom embodied in past legal decisions.

In both the case-law and code-law systems, lawyers were trained and educated essentially for the purpose of understanding and applying local, regional, royal, or national laws. There was seldom much of an intellectual attempt to understand one legal system in the context of another. In the 20th century, with improvements in transportation, the intertwining of world economics and politics, and the beginning of World War I, lawyers began to develop an interest in *international law* and in the comparative structure and workings of different legal systems around the world. Ironically, lawyers were the last to realize the potential of that field of inquiry. They had left its earliest investigations to *philosophers* and *jurists*, whose studies dated back to the ancient Greeks and had been revived during the Enlightenment, while *social* and *political scientists* had joined the research in the latter part of the 19th century. It was not until 1917 that Ernst Rabel's Institute of Comparative Law at the University of Munich became the first of its kind in the training of legal specialists. International legal studies—as opposed to a simple "Main Street" view of laws—have become particularly significant in the West, where the university training of lawyers is taken most seriously and where involvement in world affairs is keen. American lawyers, in particular, have taken a leading role in this field, emphasizing the importance of upholding individual human rights in the face of autocratic attempts to impose arbitrary legal codes.

The codification of criminal and commercial law has become a significant feature of 20th-century legal systems throughout the world, even in countries such as Great Britain and the United States, where codification has generally been scorned by lawyers, judges, and legal scholars alike. One area that has remained relatively uncodified, wide open, and extremely volatile is that of litigation. In *The Litigious Society*, published in 1981,

Jethro K. Lieberman has suggested that the preoccupation of the American bar has shifted from an earlier emphasis on cases related to the preparation and presentation of contracts, and the rights and obligations detailed therein, to cases dealing with huge monetary settlements of disputes only remotely related to actual (or sometimes even silent) contractual agreements. Such litigation as that related to *product liability, medical malpractice, environmental abuse and protection,* and *public safety and welfare* have created unlimited professional opportunities for lawyers, who are able to be original and creative in the presentation of cases that often have few precedents and limits of possible action. These lawyers must be able to realize and interpret the ramifications of *"silent" contracts,* that is, obligations that are not clearly stated in definable terms but hang loosely on such concepts as social or public responsibility. Moreover, the stakes are often exceedingly high in terms of monetary grants or court-ordered actions. This situation contrasts sharply with the history of litigation before

Attorneys often find themselves at the center of controversies, as here at the adultery trial of Rev. Henry Ward Beecher. (By J. N. Hyde, from Frank Leslie's, April 17, 1875)

the 20th century, when lawyers in *courts of equity* often sought, in response to complaints, little more than an order to cease the offense. Courts of equity rarely had the power to actually grant damages, and, consequently, the scope of legal action and the role of the lawyer in litigation cases were limited.

The legal profession has become more elite and influential in the last century than at any other time in history. Many lawyers are groomed for their careers at prestigious institutions such as the Inns of Court in England and the Ivy League colleges in America. Organizations of lawyers, such as the French *Ordre des Avocats* and many national and state bar associations around the world, often seem like exclusive clubs. Even local associations, such as metropolitan bar associations, tend to cater to their small corps of elites, who stand out against a background of lower membership. Special dress codes are frequently in effect, either overtly or otherwise. British barristers wear distinctive dark suits with white shirts; in the court itself, robes and wigs are required, even though they have been out of fashion in general society for over a century and a half. Women barristers—today comprising about 500 of the 4,000 members—are obliged to pull their hair back and wear no jewelry. They have recently rebelled against professional dress codes, especially those requiring dark—preferably black—garments to be worn along with white, long-sleeved, high-necked blouses, regardless of weather conditions, fashion trends, and so forth.

In the United States, the proliferation of lawyers has prompted one Supreme Court Justice to declare that there are just "too many lawyers." Many of these lawyers seek judicial posts as something of a career advancement. Though this type of advancement sometimes brings substantial increases in earnings, its more important benefits are prestige, public exposure, and perhaps access to political involvement. In most other countries—notably those in Europe—there are entirely separate career paths for lawyers and judges. The two are

Many young lawyers have turned their rhetorical gifts toward a career in politics. (By E. W. Kemble, from The Century Illustrated Monthly Magazine, *late 19th century)*

trained differently and licensed in what, practically, constitute different professions, and they cannot move from one profession to the other.

Besides seeking opportunities on the bench, many American lawyers turn to public rather than private practice. Some problems have emerged here, however, such as those concerning wages and working conditions, which prompted the 1980 strike of Legal Aid Society lawyers in New York City. Moreover, the overall shortage of good jobs for lawyers has created intensified competition within the field. Some law firms have opened shop in big department stores or shopping malls, offering cheaper prices and greater convenience to their clients. Lawyers in some states have recently been granted the right to compete with each other through advertising by mail—a practice condemned widely as "improper solicitation," but defended by some as the guaranteed freedom of "commercial speech."

Lawyers in Communist and Third World countries often face much more serious difficulties than clothing restrictions, limited job opportunities, or professional competition. In nations with communistic and dictatorial governments, lawyers are essentially servants of the state. As such, they are employed to represent the law, rather than the interests of private clients. Whether or not they serve the state and the law at the expense of justice and human rights has been a legal as well as political issue for some time now. The legal profession is a controversial one in authoritarian states, especially those ruled by military regimes. In such nations, lawyers are often closely identified with the ruling powers as both their puppets and protectors, and therefore share their high status. Whenever such governments are threatened with internal strife, revolution, power struggles, or even mild reforms, however, lawyers are open to sharp criticism and attack. Some may be seen as lackeys for the government, while others may be regarded as disruptive fighters for people's rights.

The Centre for the Independence of Judges and Lawyers, which makes a studied review of such developments, has frequently pointed out the precarious situation of the legal profession in authoritarian states. In Guatemala, for instance, it was estimated by the Centre that some 23 lawyers were murdered in 1980 alone. Those representing the rights of labor and equity for the poor were at the top of the hit list. Although the government disclaimed any attempts on its part to quiet reform-minded activities within the profession, one close observer noted that: "The similarity of many killings suggests a well-coordinated campaign of assassination."

The situation is not that dire in the powerful Communist countries. In China, the institution of a new, more liberal legal code in 1980 has led to an increase in the hiring of full-time lawyers in all categories of practice. Even private defense lawyers—outlawed since the Cultural Revolution of the 1960's—are suddenly very much in demand to represent the rights of clients. No shortage of lawyers exists in the Soviet Union, where those in practice are essentially state jurists and prosecutors. Defense lawyers have little opportunity of any type there. Throughout the Communist world, the activities of most lawyers are carefully watched and regulated, and channeled into some form of state service. Few members of the profession dare become involved in legal-reform movements, but those who do—besides being the objects of purge and prosecution—are also among the most influential leaders of cultural and political change.

The practice of law today takes many forms. Besides their engagement in strictly legal capacities, lawyers also act as *labor mediators*, *politicians*, *public administrators*, *business managers*, and *agents*. Some lawyers set up independent practices, while others work in partnerships or large law firms and associations. Lawyers are employed by government, business, private individuals, and large organizations such as labor unions and trade associations.

While some lawyers prey on unsuspecting individuals, making outlandish claims and promises in order to attract business, the profession has generally been associated with the protection and furtherance of human and constitutional rights. There are, within this broad scheme, controversies as to how members of the profession ought to conduct themselves and how they should be trained. Some have argued, for example, that American law schools are too much controlled by practitioners and fail to provide a balanced perspective between pure jurisprudence and actual casework. The profession may suffer from being too pragmatic and results-oriented, while overlooking the real purpose and intent of justice and legal process.

In England, solicitors have been referred to the Law Society on charges of professional misconduct and incompetence. Undue delays in settling estates, home insurance, and medical malpractice suits were the chief citations directed primarily at small-firm solicitors for plaintiffs. They were accused of taking on too many and too complex cases, frequently against large companies with better resources and more time to do justice to their side of the issue. Negligence on the part of such solicitors had reached such extremes that they were commonly taking up to 10 years to settle an estate! A full-time *Lay Observer*, also called an *ombudsman*, was finally appointed in 1974 by the Lord Chancellor to initiate appropriate reforms to alleviate these abuses. Tension between solicitors and the Lay Observer is keen, but the Observer's presence and criticism are helping to reorganize the profession and make it more accountable to the public, which may, in turn, regain its confidence in legal solicitation.

The question of fees has further complicated the issue. In 1980 the Property Transfer Association attempted to challenge the Solicitor's Act, which gives solicitors the sole authority to draw up house conveyances. The association's purpose was to avoid paying the inflated fees of the solicitors. The lawyers have managed, so far, to retain their professional privileges in this domain. But even though this and similar actions throughout the Western world have failed, they illustrate an important recent trend: the public questioning of the need for high-priced lawyers to handle simple transactions.

More than one attorney has grown testy with the restrictions of the judicial system. (From Gems From Judge, *1922)*

The legal profession is best developed and most advanced in the West, where it has two essentially distinct versions: the North American system and the European. The North American system features a profession that permits its members fluid movement between specializations and advancement primarily according to professional merit. It is a system of justice based on a broad interpretation of the law, in which custom and legal precedents are of central importance. This system applies to both the United States and Canada. In Canada the titles *barrister* and *solicitor* have been retained, but in practice both are general legal practitioners. The European system features a profession that offers very little, if any, potential movement between specializations and advancement primarily according to seniority and rank. It is a system based on a narrow interpretation of strictly codified civil laws. The British practice of law partakes of both systems.

There are many different legal specializations, and their significance varies widely, depending on whether they are part of the North American or European system. The North American *district attorney* (D.A.) prosecutes on behalf of the state in criminal cases, but offers no public or state view during private cases. The parallel practitioner in the European system is the *public prosecutor*, who likewise prosecutes criminal cases for the state but also offers an impartial opinion and public welfare analysis in private cases. By commenting on private cases, the public prosecutor actually aids the judge in the decision-making process. In Italy, public prosecutors have actually been incorporated into the judiciary.

North American government lawyers work in various government agencies and offices, while European government lawyers work in one centralized legal department that handles all legal matters for all state agencies. United States *attorneys* represent clients in court and offer them private counsel, as do European *advocates*. But while attorneys usually work in large law firms or corporations, advocates are typically found in private offices headed by a single senior member aided by only one or two *junior attorneys*. There are virtually no legal "house counsel" staffs to be found in European corporations, and legal partnerships are not only rare, but are even outlawed in some countries on the Continent.

Notary publics have little significance in the United States; they are not trained lawyers and serve only to authenticate legal documents. In Europe, though, they have considerable importance, as they actually write legal documents and operate public records offices. While European notaries maintain both public and private practices, their authority is strictly divided among notarial districts. There are few opportunities to break into this highly esteemed profession, which features tight membership regulations and influential national organizations.

Academic lawyers in the United States hold fairly secure and high-paying posts in colleges and law schools. They follow rather closely the Roman model of the jurisconsult and the medieval one of the legal philosopher, and are obliged to contribute original research and articles to the field of legal scholarship. In contrast to their academic predecessors, however, they have very close ties to the practitioners in the field. European *jurists*, meanwhile, have much more to do with actual courtroom proceedings. Their learned review of the law carries great weight in judicial decision-making, and their expertise is widely honored. Such positions are exceedingly difficult to obtain, even though they do not pay very well; those holding them often have to "moonlight" as practicing lawyers or judges in order to maintain a desired income. The economic status of academic lawyers throughout the world varies widely. At one extreme are the academic lawyers in Latin America, who can barely afford to hold their posts, despite the honor that accompanies them; at the other end of the scale are those in Germany, who have very profitable careers.

In either case, the honor and visibility of the jurist's position in the European system make it highly desirable, and apprentices are willing to endure great discomforts for the hope of obtaining it. An applicant may become an assistant to a professor of law, a position that only sometimes includes any pay at all. Once having published a book in the field, won the sponsorship or good reference of a reputable professor, and met other technical requirements, an assistant may qualify to take an admissions examination. After passing this, the new *privatdocent* is qualified to announce availability for a vacant position. Such vacancies, however, appear only rarely and are eagerly sought after by the many other qualified privatdocents. Most of them will never realize their lofty goals and are destined instead to become grateful members of some great professor's staff. From such a position, they can expect small earnings, but may enjoy the rewards of having solid professional associations and opportunities to contribute to the development of legal thought.

Whatever political system lawyers are bound by, and whether they operate within Anglo-American-style common law structures or the more typical civil law structure, they all have basic things in common. Lawyers today are usually leaders of society, who carry considerable political weight and influence. They follow demanding career paths but, if successful, may enjoy great earning potential and the respect of their social and professional peers. Moreover, they play an integral part in the maintenance and establishment of one of the most vital factors in human civilization—law.

For related occupations in this volume, *Leaders and Lawyers*, see the following:
    Judges
    Political Leaders

For related occupations in other volumes of the series, see the following:
in *Communicators* (to be published Fall 1986):
    Clerks

Scribes
Secretaries
in *Financiers and Traders*:
  Accountants and Bookkeepers
  Bankers and Financiers
  Merchants and Shopkeepers
in *Scholars and Priests* (to be published Fall 1987):
  Priests
  Scholars
  Teachers

Police and Other
Law Enforcement Officers

Civil enforcement of the law seems to have been a rare profession before the 19th century. The world's first really professional police corps—the London Metropolitan Police of Great Britain—was not established until 1829. They had some predecessors in history, however.

Civil laws and appointed *law enforcement officials* seem to have existed as early as 4000 B.C. in China and Egypt, 2,000 years before Babylonian ruler Hammurabi issued his famous codes of laws, clearly stating specific punishments for illegal actions. Ancient armies would leave a standing patrol behind them to maintain political allegiance as well as law and order in conquered nations or territories. While these patrols consisted purely of military recruits, their actual jobs often involved more policing than fighting. In that sense they may be thought of as early *police officers*.

The main distinction between police officers or law enforcers and *soldiers* is that police attempt to prevent the breaking of law or accepted standards of conduct, while soldiers are employed to engage in actual combat over an issue that is already in the stage of open hostilities. Also, police officers usually are civilians enforcing the laws of their home country, while soldiers are noncivilian—that is, part of a military establishment, separate from civilian life—who most typically enforce international law. These are rule-of-thumb distinctions, however, and do not apply so neatly to ancient and medieval societies as they do to modern ones.

The first civil law enforcers that we have definite knowledge of were the *ephori* of ancient Sparta. They were a body of five elected officials who wielded almost limitless power in the enforcement of both law and proper moral conduct. They acted as a combination of *investigator*, *judge*, *jury*, and *executioner*. They carried out the decrees of the legislation, supervised education, levied fines, and meted out punishments. The ephori were an isolated example, however; distinct civil law enforcers

Early watchmen were not professionals but citizens taking "watch and ward" duty on a rotating basis. (From The Book of Days, *1864)*

were not generally found elsewhere in either ancient Greece or Rome. In Imperial Rome military officers called *lictors* were specifically charged with maintaining order, and there may have been a small corps of civilians employed in the policing of city streets.

The roots of the police profession as we know it today lie in ninth-century England, where the Anglo-Saxons first organized their population for military protection under King Alfred. Each group of 100 people were to elect a *reeve* as their leader. Several such groups together chose a *shire*. While the responsibilities of the reeve and the shire were originally related to military concerns, these officials were, in fact, elected civilians. Eventually the two jobs were combined into one *shire-reeve*, later to be known by the more familiar term, *sheriff*. The shire-reeve became the chief judicial and law enforcement officer in each county. The position soon became so powerful that it could be obtained only through appointment by the royal crown.

After the 1066 Norman Conquest of England, the system of sheriffs was retained in order to ensure public safety, but sheriffs became much more than civilian protectors. They also received military status. Their positions were of high rank, usually going to landed barons and being handed down from father to son. In addition to the old system, the Normans added *night watches* to protect the public from crime and violence while they slept. Every male 16 years old and over was obliged to stand "watch and ward" duty on a rotating schedule. All *watchmen* were expected to join forces in response to a "hue and cry" calling forth a *posse comitatus*—a chase after a person fleeing the town after just committing a crime.

The sheriffs were powerful professionals in Norman England. Aided by his watchmen, a sheriff was empowered to bring *criminals* to trial. The sheriff also presided over the trial and passed sentence. To handle such a large job, the sheriffs of the larger counties began the practice of hiring a full-time *Comes Stabuli*

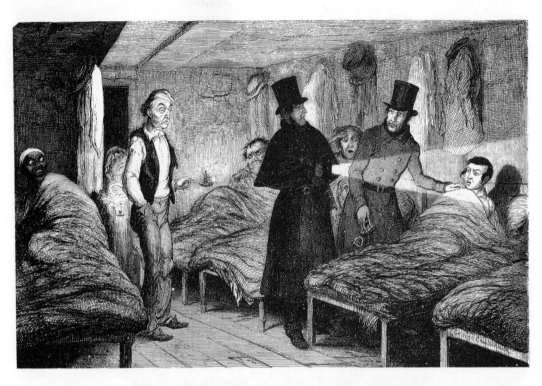

In the rougher sections of cities, police officers went in pairs to apprehend criminals. (By George Cruikshank, from The Drunkard's Children: A Sequel to the Bottle, *1848)*

(*constable*) as an assistant. In 1072 circuit court *judges* appeared on the scene, relieving the sheriff and constable of their judicial authority. Thereafer, the chief duty of both sheriff and constable was to see that the king received enough profits from the people (through taxation and fines) so that he would not consider appointing others to those offices.

For the most part, the sheriff and constable were much more concerned with crimes against the crown than those against private persons or merchants. Concerning such matters as *burglary* or *assault*, private individuals had little protection, unless they were affluent enough to hire private police protection. In 1166 King Henry II, who became known as "the Law-Giver," issued the *Leges Henrici*, which obliged law enforcers to protect the public. This edict had little practical influence on the system at that time, but it set important legal precedent concerning the government's obligation to protect its citizens against crime as well as foreign invasion. It was this precedent that eventually led to the establishment of modern police forces.

In 1285 King Edward I established a *curfew* for the city of Westminster (then capital of England). The city gates were closed at night so that only city residents remained within, while undesirables were locked out. To enforce this curfew and other special nighttime rules, Edward created a night watch with *bailiffs*, who were responsible for guarding the city gates. All citizens had to serve in turn, but a small salary was provided. The king's bailiffs seem to have had a morale problem, however, for they were constantly being reprimanded for sleeping on the job. A special branch of the night watch, the *Police Desmour*, patrolled the streets. Among their various responsibilities was making sure that *prostitutes* were confined to their designated "business" districts. In the 14th century the police patrols were given job training for the first time. The position of shire-reeve was replaced by that of *justice of the peace*, which was a law enforcement job for almost a century, before it became a purely judicial post.

The government services still supplied little protection for individuals, however. So from the 14th century until the 19th, law and order fell increasingly into the hands of *private police*. These were basically of two types: the *market police*, hired by merchants for the protection of their property and the recovery of stolen goods, and the *parochial police*, hired by church communities to protect church members and property. The market and parochial police were under no control of or obligation to the government. Only the *military police* were, and they were little more than *watchmen* and *wards* as far as protecting the general public was concerned. Even as late as 1737, the city of London had only 68 paid patrol officers—30 for daytime duty, 38 for nighttime.

The Industrial Revolution had its greatest early impact in England and later in the United States. It is no coincidence that the history of the police profession before the 20th century is confined mostly to these two countries.

It was the new industrialized cities—and the problems they spawned—that finally made the medieval "watch and ward" system obsolete. Poverty, famine, looting, and rioting became widespread in these new centers of mass production as hordes of poor people from rural areas moved to the cities and failed to find the prosperity they had hoped would be theirs. Thousands of "street urchins"—small, homeless children who stole to survive—pestered decent citizens in the marketplaces, while general vagrancy, burglary, and violent crime rose to astounding levels.

In 1829 Sir Robert Peel, a member of Parliament, proposed the creation of a professional police force for the Greater London metropolitan area. He insisted that the watch and ward was completely ineffective to stem the tide of increasing crime in that district. The old system of ill-paid volunteers had, over the centuries, given way to a system of ill-paid substitutes, as volunteers hired others to stand the night watch in their stead. Robert Peel sarcastically called it the "shiver and shake watch," explaining that its recruits spent half the night shivering from the cold, and the other half shaking from fear. The London Metropolitan Police, with headquarters at Scotland Yard, was established as the world's first fully professional police force. Officers were screened carefully for the 1,000-man force. Many applied but few were accepted.

After Peel put the trainees through rigorous physical training and harsh discipline, many quit. But Peel insisted that he wanted no weeds, only flowers. Officers had to undergo a probationary period and subject themselves to periodic review. They wore top hats and tailcoats, but were not allowed to be armed in the early years of the force's history, since too many members of Parliament feared armed rebellion of the type that had led to the French and other Continental revolutions. There was a high turnover in personnel for the first few years, but by 1835 Peel had fully organized an efficient and well-trained police force.

Smaller cities and towns did not immediately benefit from the operations at Scotland Yard. In 1834 Liverpool was considered "the blackspot on the Mersey" because it had only 50 watchmen to protect a population of 250,000. Hull was one of the first towns to create a police force, in 1835. The chief constable and 39 policemen were paid according to the number of arrests they made: their motto was "no prisoner, no pay." The busy seaport cities had always bred high levels of crime, but it was not until the mid-1830's—when a group called the Chartists posed a direct threat of revolution against the government—that paid and armed police were allowed to serve outside of London district. By 1856 the government absolutely required every town to maintain a police force, for which it would help pay for uniforms and salaries. The profession began to swell in numbers and to improve in terms of both financial security and prestige. *Bobbies*, or *peelers*, as the London police were affectionately named, after Sir Robert Peel, even got uniforms and helmets in 1867 to replace the top hats and tails.

The job was no easy one. Police had a wide variety of duties in 19th-century England. They worked rotating shifts of 12 hours—either day or night. They rarely had days off, even during holidays, since they were the sole protectors of the public safety, and budgets made little allowance for substitutes. They were especially obliged to make sure that business could be carried on without fear. Most markets contained substantial lots of goods sold from open-air carts, baskets, and shipping crates on the walkways outside of shops. These goods wee particularly inviting to *thieves* and street urchins. The task of protecting the wares of these merchants was extremely difficult. Almost as difficult was the job of safeguarding shoppers from *pickpockets*, often street urchins who were nearly impossible to catch as they scampered away into the dark alleyways.

Controlling theater crowds was another responsibility of city police. In many towns police officers also had to take charge of putting out fires, although in larger cities they were spared this dangerous job. Police officers were directly charged with the public welfare, and in this capacity they did things such as operating a handcart type of ambulance to transport the injured or sick to a hospital, and the inebriated to Police Court. They also had to tend to a certain amount of paperwork. Each officer had to file *route papers* on his daily routine. These included reports of crime, accidents, and missing persons. The reports were then carried to different stations in all the precincts and even to nearby towns for information files or follow-up action and alerts. Each morning, night duty patrol officers reported to Police Court with arrested criminals, prostitutes, and lost or starving children who had been rounded up during the previous night's tour of duty.

Each patrol officer had a specific *beat*, or area to be responsible for. This might include troublesome market and theater districts, as well as the truly dangerous spots such as seaport and river-front dockyards, and drinking and gambling districts. But while patrol officers spent considerable effort protecting the merchant squares, they seldom ventured near the districts where truly serious and violent crimes were commonplace. When they did, they went in teams, to raid cockfighting or drinking establishments, for example. Otherwise they largely stayed clear of the places frequented by cutthroat *highwaymen*, hardened criminals, and violent drunkards and *gamblers*. In addition to beats on the streets, regular *river police* traveled up and down busy commercial waterways on patrol boats. A *mounted police* force was also available to go into territories where the terrain was particularly rough, in order to ferret out outlaws and hideaways.

While the London police force was being whipped into an efficient and tightly operating unit, a special detective force called the Bow Street Runners was also being created. This organization was actually a throwback to earlier times, when the Bow Street Runners had been a professional organization of ruthless *bounty hunters*, who

Police officers, sometimes assisted by soldiers, are called on to quell civil disorder, as in New York's Civil War Draft Riots. (From Harper's Weekly, *August 1, 1863*)

received high rewards for bringing in wanted criminals, either dead or alive. Under the direction of Scotland Yard, the new Bow Street Runners were molded into one of the first professional *detective* forces. They differed from regular police officers in many ways. Their job was to investigate crimes that had been committed without clear evidence as to the exact circumstances of and parties to the illegality. All Bow Street Runners were *plainclothes officers*. That is, they wore no uniforms and tried to conceal their profession in order to gain the confidence of unwitting informers. They were used as *decoys* and *plants*, infiltrating groups about which more precise information was needed to determine the nature and extent of their suspected criminal activity. Nonetheless, it was apparently rather easy for the backstreeters of Victorian England to distinguish between their legitimate brothers in crime and the thinly disguised detectives.

The Bow Street Runners continued as a detective force for about 10 years. No new officers were appointed and the organization became extinct, leaving only the peelers to investigate crime. The peelers proved inept at this job, however, and an eight-man Detective Force was created.

It, too, had a difficult time for a while, as did the other newly forming detective departments in France and the United States. One of the original members of the Detective Force resigned after having apparently accused a woman of a murder without properly developing his case. As it turned out, however, the woman eventually went to a convent, where she confessed her crime and was subsequently arrested. There were many other blunders, though, that did not turn out so well. There was also considerable popular resentment against the idea of plainclothes police lurking about and snooping into everyone's business. An 1845 article in *Punch* typifies the nature of the controversy:

Its [the Detective Force's] members, disguised in plain clothes, are now known to mix in all societies, to whose manners and peculiarities they are instructed to adapt themselves. They mingle, as exquisites, in the "salons" of fashion; they creep, as cads, into the "crib" of the costermonger. They frequent every species of tavern, from the first rate to the Jerry-shop; and neither the freedom of the tap nor the sanctity of the parlour is safe from their intrusion...But the evil does not stop here. In his uniform the Policeman is notorious for scraping acquaintances with servants at area railings...How much longer are free born Englishmen to submit to the espionage and to be victimised by the voracity of...[a snooping detective]?

It must be remembered that in 1845 the idea of a civil police force was a radically new one, and to give the force the advantage of secrecy was too much for many to accept.

After another serious blunder by the force and its inspectors (there were originally two inspectors aided by six sergeants) in 1876, it was completely reorganized by Scotland Yard into the Criminal Investigation Department (CID). Thereafter, job training became much more rigorous and scientific. For the first time, detectives were trained in basic law, so that their evidence and accusations might have a better chance of standing up in court. *The Police Code and Manual of the Criminal Law* was printed in a pocket-size version so that it could be readily referred to by both detectives and patrol officers. From that time to this, the police and detective professions have become increasingly complex and scientific, so that we now speak of *police science* as the standard curriculum of professional training.

The London law enforcement team was the first and the most widely copied system in the world. But police systems were developing elsewhere, too, notably in the United States. In North America, the English developments in public safety were generally followed. In 1636 Boston had civilian watchmen as well as military guards. In New Amsterdam (now New York City) watchmen were called the *rattel wacht*, because they carried rattles, which they shook when they needed assistance from a nearby fellow watchman. In 1658 the voluntary *rattel wacht* was replaced by a paid force of eight patrolmen.

In 1844 New York City created a professional police force, which used London's as its model. It included a united day and night force, as Peel had recommended. Previously the city's Day Watch was completely separate from its Night Watch. Patrol officers were called *cops* or *coppers*—either after the abbreviation for "constable on patrol" (C.O.P.) or because the first recruits wore an eight-point copper star, or both. In addition to large city police forces, the United States had elected county sheriffs and constables, while the federal *U.S. Marshal* was in charge of protecting the sparsely populated territories.

Police forces in the United States tended to be quite corrupt before the 20th century. Part of the problem was that *chiefs of police* were elected to short terms. As a result, these positions were usually held on only a part-time basis by less-than-totally-committed *shopkeepers* or *business owners* who often only sought the office to benefit their own business concerns. They were easily won over by politicians and wealthy merchants, who frequently requested special favors. Eventually the post of chief was converted into a full-time professional one, while *police boards* were created to help in administration. But politicians controlled both chiefs and boards. Even patrol officers—grossly overworked and underpaid—generated constant complaints (apparently well-documented) of corruption and brutality.

Also closely modeled on the British system was the Canadian one. In 1835 Toronto became the first city in Canada with a professional police force. It had a *chief constable* and five police officers. In 1873 the Northwest Mounted Police was formed to protect westward-bound pioneers and settlers. Now called the Royal Canadian Mounted Police, it is one of the most highly regarded law enforcement organizations in the world.

The French created one of the finest detective forces in the world in the 19th century. It was so successful that it was even copied by the British Criminal Investigation Department. The French also established one of the most efficient and highly regarded rural police organizations, manned by the highly disciplined *gendarmes*. Paris developed a British-style law enforcement agency. Its officers were called *agents de police*, or more commonly, *flics*. Italy's police system, essentially paramilitary, featured the efficient *carabinieri*.

The 20th century has seen profound changes in the development of the police profession. Technology has improved the efficiency of both patrol officers and detectives. New forms of transportation have been readily adapted by police personnel. Cars, scooters, boats, and helicopters are all commonly in use today. Radios, telephones, photographic equipment, and computers have made possible rapid communication between officers, between officers and their stations, between stations over the vast expanses of entire nations, and even between nations. Crime investigators use computers to process fingerprints and to make criminal files readily available for inspection. "Image-maker" or "image-reflector" machines may be manually operated by police personnel to arrange a graphic image of a suspected criminal based on eyewitness accounts. These pictures may then be printed and widely distributed to stations all over the city, county, nation, or world.

In the mid-20th century, police personnel have made great advances in financial security, working conditions, public image, and social status. It was not long ago that 12-hour days were considered normal in the profession, with few days off for any reason. Today, the 8-hour day is typical, with liberal sick pay and holiday pay in addition to regular days off. Rotating shifts between day, evening, and night are one aspect of the job that many officers do not especially care for, but are usually saddled with. Salaries have improved greatly in the United States and Great Britain, so that they are now at least on a par with other middle-class jobs. Salaries are comparatively lower in continental Europe, although personnel there are frequently given additional housing provisions or rent allowances.

In the early 19th century the very notion of a professional police force to protect and control society was repugnant to the general public. For many years after, the blundering and scandal within the profession heightened people's misgivings about police forces. Today, though, officers of the law enjoy considerable—though still guarded—social esteem and respect. This change in the public attitude is the result of police use of technology to improve performance and efficiency; better programs of police training and steadily improving techniques of patrolling and investigation; and—especially in the United States—greater independence of the metropolitan police administration boards from politicians.

Corruption and brutality within the profession have generally declined as the status of the profession has improved. In the United States, where such problems were particularly acute before the 20th century, improvement came when strong and upright individuals began to obtain positions as commissioners of large city forces. Theodore Roosevelt was one such leader who was determined to make the force respectable and responsible. Political patronage (the awarding of jobs to a successful politician's supporters) in the occupation finally eroded when the merit system came into general use for placement of police personnel.

Aspiring police officers have always had to meet certain physical requirements. Traditionally most have been male. But the first policewoman in the United States was appointed to the New York City police department in 1888. The British have allowed women in the profession for about the same length of time. Most countries have only recently admitted women, however. The first Frenchwoman in the profession was employed in 1963, and some countries still have no women on their police rosters. Minority group members, such as Blacks, have faced similar difficulties in most Western countries.

Beyond physical qualifications for acceptance into police work, training has become an important and universal prerequisite. August Vollmer—once the police chief of Berkeley, California, and often considered the father of modern police work—introduced the practice of requiring recruits to have a general college degree in addition to special professional training. In England, recruits attend the Peel House or the National Police School or both. There is also national police force training in Canada, but in most other countries police training is handled by the military establishment, which is, in turn, controlled by the central government. In the United States, training schools and academies are usually operated by individual cities, often in conjunction with local colleges and universities. The Federal Bureau of Investigation (FBI) in Washington, D.C., operates the National Academy, which trains teachers for metropolitan police training academies. In this very indirect manner, the federal government has some hand in the shaping of local police force organizations.

Police personnel are not directly represented by any labor unions, but in England and North America they have formed *benevolent* and *protective organizations*, which sometimes seem to act like unions. After the

British police strike of 1919, a federation of English and Welsh officers was formed. The government agreed to consult the Police Federation before making any policy decisions affecting the law enforcement profession. In countries where police forces are military or paramilitary in nature, there is little chance for officers to organize in this way. On the other hand, it is not uncommon in countries with unstable governments (usually Third World countries) for police forces to militarily support, and sometimes even to organize, political revolutions. In democratic nations, where laborers are typically free to organize and strike, law enforcement officers are excluded from this right. The argument offered by the central government in such cases is that domestic order and public safety cannot be jeopardized by labor disputes. Police personnel in democratic countries are usually offered hearings concerning their complaints, however, and many disputes are eventually heard and ruled on by *arbitration boards* and committees.

In many industrialized countries, job security in the field has been somewhat diminished recently because of the worldwide recession. As city budgets become overwhelming and taxpayers cry out for relief, many authorities cut back on financial support for police organizations, forcing the indefinite laying off of many officers. Yet, the need for protection against criminals still exists.

Many police forces, in an attempt to overcome this dilemma, have tried to become more sophisticated and less labor-intensive. They have increased their use of computers and technology to replace long work hours, as well as to update patrol communications and transportation. Of course, new technology does not compensate for the loss of patrol officers on the streets. Some forces have tried using officers on single patrols, rather than in teams of two. Others now use specially trained police dogs to work with officers. Still others operate active community relations programs. These programs seek to educate citizens to assist the police in doing their job, to make better use of police services, and to teach people how to avoid creating situations in which they might become vulnerable to crime.

In some cities today, citizens have formed civilian groups that actively help the police patrol neighborhoods. Some of these are coordinated by the police department and actually form voluntary *auxiliary police* units. Others are organized independently and are often denounced by police personnel as impeding the professional law enforcers in carrying out their duties to protect the people. The latter groups are very much like the voluntary *vigilante groups* that have been formed in many places throughout the ages, when there was thought to be a lack of adequate protection by authorized law enforcement agencies. Vigilante groups of citizens characterized the pioneer settlement of North America, as its boundaries were pushed westward into the wilderness. Many of those groups not only sought out and arrested suspected outlaws but also tried and sentenced them—sometimes right on the spot and usually with little regard for the rights of the accused.

Although Frederick Douglass was appointed U. S. Marshal of the District of Columbia, minorities were ill-represented in the police until recent years. (From Frank Leslie's Illustrated Weekly)

Police forces are usually organized according to rank. In the United States, for example, municipal police forces are headed by a *police commissioner*. Under the commissioner are the *captains* of the individual precincts (police districts). Under the captains are the *lieutenants*, *sergeants*, and *patrol officers*. In addition to this basic structure, there are also detective forces of plainclothes officers. These are usually designated by the specific departments in which they specialize, as for example, *homicide detectives* or *narcotics agents*. There are also *police surgeons* appointed to precincts. They treat job-related injuries and investigate the nature of them, for the purpose of advising insurance and pension boards.

In the United States each county has an elected sheriff, whose duties may range from controlling large forces of deputies to simply watching the jailhouse. Small towns may have only a *marshal* or *constable* to look after their safety and protection. There are also *state police* in each of the nation's individual states. Tracing their roots back to vigilante-style groups such as the early Texas Rangers, the first professional *state troopers* were employed strictly to supervise traffic control on state roadways. The first such organization was formed by the State of Pennsylvania in 1905. State troopers today play a major role in all aspects of professional law enforcement.

Modern police forces have many special *task forces*. The members of these forces are usually police personnel with advanced training in special areas. Such training makes them more valuable, gives them more prestige as professionals, and allows them to earn more money. Usually, however, these special jobs also entail a substantially higher risk. Training of task force personnel is sometimes done through special programs operated by police or military academies or by federal government agencies. Sometimes it is accomplished partly through on-the-job training programs. Some typical types of special forces are *hostage negotiating teams*, *terrorist control* and *prevention teams*, *crowd control forces*, *motorcycle squads*, *bomb squads*, and *vice squads*.

At the highest level, plainclothes law enforcers and crime investigators are employed by the federal government. *Federal Bureau of Investigation (FBI) agents* protect the government against crimes and frauds involving currency, narcotics, federal taxes, customs procedures and revenues, immigration, and the mails. They are especially well-trained in investigating organized crime and terrorist groups, who pose a threat to the legal sanctity and even security of the nation. *Secret service officers*, meanwhile, provide personal protection for the president and vice-president and their families, as well as for foreign diplomats and their families residing in the nation's capital.

The nature of the police profession in different countries around the world varies most notably according to the amount of government control over it. Many central governments control all levels and activities of their law enforcement organizations. The Gestapo of Nazi Germany and the Oura of Mussolini's Italy are good historical examples of so-called *secret police* agencies. These types of organizations are found today in the Soviet Union (which operates the highly publicized KGB), the People's Republic of China, and some Third World countries. Officers in these services are less concerned with the prevention of crime than with the prosecution of offenders. In particular, they seek to prosecute political offenders, anyone seen as a threat to the image or security of the government in power. This function generally takes precedence over the control of crime against ordinary citizens. Secret police are almost always military personnel, controlled directly by the government.

Other countries have paramilitary police forces. These include the *carabinieri* of Italy and the French *gendarmes*. They are essentially military personnel who are in charge of enforcing civil laws and protecting the public. Many Third World countries also feature this sort of police profession. In *police states*, where political leadership is formed and retained by military might rather than by democratic electoral systems, military or paramilitary officers may be called upon to act as soldiers for or against the standing government.

England, Canada, and the United States provide the best examples of police forces that are essentially free of control by the central government. Of these, the United States easily has the most independent police profession, although local police forces do coordinate to some extent with the Federal Bureau of Investigation and the various state governments. While the U.S. system now serves as a model for democratic nations, it has been more prone to corruption, vice, and local politics than those systems coordinated more closely by strong central governments and their agencies. The American law enforcement system also creates often conflicting sources of authority. For example, the courts, which have increasingly acted to protect the civil rights of accused parties, are sometimes seen by police officers as undermining the effective execution of law enforcement.

This Chinese police officer is leading a prisoner by a chain around his neck, in addition to those on his ankles. (From The New America and the Far East; *by G. Waldo Browne, 1901)*

Police also protect; these homeless people are spending the winter's night on the floor of the precinct house. (By Winslow Homer, from Harper's Weekly, *February 7, 1874)*

At the international level, over 100 nations contribute to a crime prevention and law enforcement organization called the *International Criminal Police Organization*, better known as *Interpol*. First established in 1923, with headquarters in Vienna, it was dissolved by Hitler in the early stages of World War II, but reestablished in 1946 with new headquarters in Paris. Interpol keeps files on international criminals and assists member nations in locating them, although it is not directly responsible for apprehending criminals. The agency educates its members about the latest scientific techniques of crime investigation and prevention. Interpol has been particularly successful in the prevention and detection of international counterfeiting, smuggling, and narcotics dealing.

For related occupations in this volume, *Leaders and Lawyers*, see the following:
Lawyers
Judges
Political Leaders
Prison Guards and Executioners
Secret Police

For related occupations in other volumes of the series, see the following:

in *Communicators* (to be published Fall 1986):
    Messengers and Couriers
in *Helpers and Aides* (to be published Spring 1987):
    Firefighters
in *Healers* (to be published Spring 1987):
    Nurses
    Physicians and Surgeons
in *Performers and Players* (to be published Fall 1987):
    Animal Trainers
in *Scientists and Technologists* (to be published Spring 1988):
    Computer Scientists
in *Restaurateurs and Innkeepers* (to be published Spring 1988):
    Innkeepers
in *Warriors and Adventurers* (to be published Spring 1988):
    Gamblers and Gamesters
    Prostitutes
    Robbers and Other Criminals
    Soldiers
    Spies

Political Leaders

Political leadership has been one of the most important and influential occupations since the beginning of civilization. From the time that human beings first joined together in groups, leaders of some sort existed. Why and how people become leaders or rulers in human society is a matter of much discussion among sociologists, anthropologists, psychologists, and historians. Some people who become rulers are driven by the desire to acquire power; others wish to amass wealth and prestige; still others desire to help shape institutions and legislation that will affect other peoples' lives. Often, of course, leaders are motivated by some combination of these ambitions. Many psychological studies of *political leaders* have tried to determine just what drives a person into so rigorous and competitive a career—for probably no career is more demanding. Yet no simple stereotype of the political leader has emerged showing similar ambitions or personal characteristics.

Many political leaders throughout history have, of course, been groomed for the job. Perhaps because the qualities and skills needed for political leadership are so many and varied, people who have learned about ruling firsthand are often thought best prepared for the work. So, at some early stage, there developed a pattern of political leaders being drawn from among the ruling family, or from among a few aristocratic families. The position of political leader was often passed down within a family, from father or mother to son or daughter; or, on the death of an old leader, a new one might be chosen from among the strongest candidates within a few families grouped around the throne.

Every society has had to face the problem of succession—the need to find a new leader upon the loss of an old one. The problem is that, if the leadership is passed automatically within a single ruling family, the community faces the possibility of a weak ruler, for not all

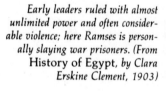

Early leaders ruled with almost unlimited power and often considerable violence; here Ramses is personally slaying war prisoners. (From History of Egypt, *by Clara Erskine Clement, 1903)*

who grow up near the throne are prepared to rule effectively. On the other hand, if the new leader is to be selected from among several candidates, the community faces the prospect of dividing into factions, each supporting a different candidate, so the community might be weakened. Often, of course, a new leader takes over as a result of military conquest, especially when a society is temporarily leaderless. These questions of succession have never been solved entirely satisfactorily and plague humanity to this day. They are all the more important because political leaders have played such a central role in shaping history and developing the institutions by which we all live.

Throughout much of human history, political leaders have had almost unlimited power once in office. They have held the power to make laws, to interpret them, and to enforce them. In the earliest cosmopolitan civilizations of the Egyptians, Mesopotamians, Hittites, and Chinese, rulers and their positions were often thought to have a divine origin. Although *kings* and *queens* sometimes came to power through military force or conquest, it was firmly believed that they could do so only if they had the favor of the gods. The Egyptians even believed that the pharaoh himself was a god. Under such circumstances it is hardly surprising that the ancient *monarchs* had absolute authority to make decrees, pass laws, and formulate foreign policy as they wished. All citizens were their humble subjects, with no power or right to do anything about royal orders except to obey them.

While ancient kings had absolute authority in all matters, they found it convenient and necessary to delegate some of it to others whom they personally appointed. So there developed, very early on, a political hierarchy, ranks of government *officials* who served the king. Positions in the hierarchy were filled mostly by persons of noble birth and many were essentially hereditary. The jobs were retained by winning over and maintaining the favor of the royal family and those immediate superiors who could recommend selections and dismissals of various officials. Most of the positions were created to see to it that royal edicts were obeyed and that taxes or other obligations were faithfully remitted. These early government officials were essentially *law enforcement officers*, *inspectors* of various products and practices, and *collectors* of taxes and foreign revenues. (These revenues were often exacted in the form of *tributes* paid regularly from the treasuries of conquered territories or tribes.) Early officials were not political leaders as such. Occasionally, an official with a powerful personality and outstanding ability could gain some real influence, but in general they had little or nothing to say about domestic legislation, foreign affairs, business or commercial policies, or even the structure of the government.

It is not surprising that these court officials had little legislative power, for there were very few standardized or codified laws in early times. Most laws came directly from the king or queen and were strictly spontaneous, arising out of a specific situation but not intended to have general application. Then, in the 18th century B.C. the Babylonian King Hammurabi issued his famous Code of Hammurabi, a comprehensive set of standardized laws. The code of Hammurabi set a very important precedent, which many other monarchs followed. Laws became more clear and concise, so that citizens and government officials alike would not be confused as to what constituted an illegal act, and what the punishment for breaking the law would be. The rise of standardized laws gave some sense of continuity to legal tradition, made government more manageable, and made lawmaking duties a more important activity of rulers and their corps of political advisors and court officials. Still, legislative bodies as such did not really exist in any significant form before the Classical age of Greece.

Ancient rulers had two formidable opponents to their authority. The first was the *priesthood*. This opposition may seem odd, since early kings were usually leaders of the temple as well as the palace. Rival priesthoods would

During Classical times, senators like these Romans had power during brief republican periods. (From Men: A Pictorial Archive From Nineteenth-Century Sources, *by Jim Harter, Dover, 1980)*

arise, however, based on their worship of different patron gods. Religion, therefore, was often the cause of bitter political confrontations. This is not to say that there was only room for the worship of one god, but rather that only one god could assume the top political position at any given time. What developed, then, was a sort of religious *political party system.* Seldom was there any attempt to unite the various temples under one king, because the opposing priesthoods themselves were too powerful to be so controlled by a single central authority. One such ambitious plan was undertaken during Egypt's 18th dynasty. It was then, in the 14th century B.C., that Ikhnaton united the entire kingdom under the sun god Aton. Ikhnaton's religious idea of worshiping one god dissipated quickly after his death, but his political notion of a strong central rulership was carried on by his successor Tutankhamen, better known to many as "King Tut." He established a strong code of laws, as Hammurabi had done several hundred years earlier, and even a *judiciary* branch to interpret the laws.

In ancient kingdoms, successful rulers usually had to have the support of the major religious cults and their leading *priests*. Beyond this, they also had to maintain a strong standing army, for the second greatest challenge to their authority was the foreign rulers who sought to conquer or exact tribute from their kingdoms. Ancient leaders were constantly at war in an attempt to expand their empires, to avoid being conquered themselves, or to put down internal rebellions. Therefore they had to be strong military leaders as well as religious leaders. Chinese rulers were thought to have the "mandate of Heaven"—a divinely given right to rule, as long as they were able to hold together the empire through a strong and capable central government that was, in turn, able to provide protection for its people.

Ancient rulers had nearly complete authority over matters of government, religion, education, and commerce. While expanding their empires and kingdoms, however, they found it necessary to appoint lesser political leaders as *governors* of outlying territories. By standardizing and codifying laws, moreover, they paved the way for what would eventually become another new class of political leaders—*legislators*. In attempting to maintain an informed leadership over increasingly complex societies and their governments, they also selected special *advisors* to keep them abreast of changing political situations and to help them make critical decisions. In some cases, court advisors became so powerful and trusted that they may be considered to have been leaders of the state in fact, if not in name.

Such political leaders in this period were almost always appointed; their positions were frequently won through favor and passed on to their offspring. They were, therefore, an elite class and had little incentive to represent the needs of the general population. Except in isolated cases, they used their power only to help themselves and their influential friends. Whatever they did for the general public was only to pacify it and to make the most efficient use of it—usually in terms of military ventures, agricultural production, and public works projects. The greatest initiative in forming new policies and trying to improve outdated systems of governing came from the monarchs themselves or occasionally from a farsighted chief advisor. Political leadership remained concentrated in a very small elite group for many centuries.

A sudden break with this traditional arrangement came in early Greece. For many years Greek city-states had been ruled by *tyrants* or kings. These tyrants did not enjoy the status of gods, as did the Egyptian pharaohs, nor did they rule with the "mandate of Heaven" that Chinese kings had. They were often little more than military personnel who held short terms of power until they could be overthrown. Some of the tyrants were somewhat enlightened and tried to foster some stability by establishing laws and seeking political advice from a few prominent nobles. But their attempts to establish long-standing hereditary dynasties like those of the ancient Near and Far East were dismal failures. The constant changing of political leadership, and therefore of laws and general political policies, created great confusion and continual internal strife and civil disruption.

From this background emerged two powerful city-states that established new ideas of political leadership. Sparta and Athens both created societies that were more democratic than any ever before known. They did away with the position of a single tyrant with sole authority in all matters, and tried to divide such power among a greater number of political leaders and representatives.

The Spartan model was essentially one of aristocratic control of the state, what we might now call an *oligarchy*. The office of the tyrant was replaced by two kings and 28 elders, who together formed the upper house of a *bicameral* legislature (one with two houses). The lower house was composed of citizens over the age of 30; the upper house initiated legislation, but the lower house had to approve it. The executive and judicial powers of this

From early times Chinese rulers employed the services of a great bureaucracy of scholars and administrators. (From The New America and the Far East, *by G. Waldo Browne, 1901, from a Korean temple painting)*

government were combined into a single unit. Called the *ephorate*, it had five magistrates (*ephors*) who had the power to interpret the law, enforce it, and exact punishment for offenses.

The system may sound democratic, and by ancient standards it was. In modern terms, it was more an oligarchy, however, because membership to both the legislature and the ephorate was severely restricted to landed aristocrats, who monopolized the power and prestige of ancient Spartan society. Moreover, the ephors soon became so powerful that, for all practical purposes, they ran the government to their liking. They probed into every aspect of Spartan life, including moral conduct and religious and educational practices. They even supervised the lives of the legislators, and soon took over their duties, in effect. The ephors were elected to their posts each year, but Spartans eligible to vote came from a very small and elite group, so that political leadership rested on a very narrow base.

Sparta's political system was not a true democracy, but it did prove to be quite efficient for the running of Sparta's militaristic society. Furthermore, it was quite liberal when compared with hereditary and absolutist tyrannies and dynasties ruled over by one person and succeeding generations of offspring. The five elected ephors all had an equal voice in decision-making, and they even kept a close eye on one another's public and personal conduct.

The Athenians went even further than the Spartans in restructuring the nature and scope of political leadership. In the early seventh century B.C. they abolished the monarchy. A hundred years later some democratic reforms were initiated by Solon. Around 500 B.C. Cleisthenes refined the system even further, giving Athens the first truly democratic government and one that would serve as a model ever after. Basically, it revolved around a system that incorporated the popular election of *representatives* to the legislature.

The Athenian population was divided into 10 tribes, each of which could send 50 representatives to the *boule*,

Europe's Holy Roman Emperors considered themselves in direct line from Julius Caesar. (By Jost Amman, from The Book of Trades, late 16th century)

or council of 500. The boule would initiate legislation and make policy decisions, which then had to be ratified by the *ecclesia*, the popular assembly. Members of the ecclesia were drawn from the general citizenry; this assembly quickly came to be dominated by the middle class. Other city-states, however, feared the revolutionary concept of democracy being tried out by the Athenians. Aristocrats from several of them tried to band together with Athenian aristocrats to overthrow the liberal experiment, but it survived for many years.

The resounding message of the Greek's broad conception of political leadership was that government ought not be controlled by a single individual or even by too small a group of rulers. Leadership became much more a public matter than it ever had been before. Beyond this general principle there also arose the specific idea of a legislature that was separate from the executive and judiciary bodies. Previously it had always been assumed that the head ruler of the state should decree the laws and then see to it that they were obeyed and properly interpreted. Greek governments typically separated this authority, thereby extending the concept of political leadership beyond the crown or military ruler. Government now included representatives from more factions of society—most typically the aristocratic and middle classes, but sometimes even commoners to a limited degree. It might have been expected that from this point on governments would become increasingly democratic, but this was not to be the case. Roman armies soon invaded the Greek mainland. The Romans incorporated the culture and political institutions of the Greeks into their own, but they made drastic revisions based on an entirely different view of the political nature of society.

While the Greeks thought that government was created to make society prosperous, harmonious, and efficient, the Romans held to a more traditional view. They believed that government was created for the proper management of conquered lands and peoples, and the maintenance of a social balance among classes, so that all

Medieval leaders derived much of their power from the church; here Pope Clement IV gives the Kingdom of Naples to Charles of Anjou. (French Embassy Press and Information Division, 13th century)

members of society knew their place. An even deeper philosophical division underlay the issue, however. The Greeks felt that people should pursue an active course of investigation that would help them better understand the actions of the gods and the nature of the universe. Based on this knowledge, they might then endeavor to strike a balance between society and nature and create a state whose main goal would be the peaceful coexistence of the two.

There was, of course, no Greek nation, but rather many separate city-states. Controversy raged among them as to how far such an idealistic concept should be taken. Athens was the crowning example of the ideal state, rooted in democracy and with its chief vision the pursuit of knowledge, beauty, understanding, and balance with the forces of nature and the supernatural. The Romans were much more like the Spartans. They condemned the Athenian attitude as weak and impractical. The Romans thought people should conquer nature, use the gods for the benefit of their own progress, and mold the universe into exactly what they wanted. The very fact that the

Roman military machine was able to roll over the Greeks on the battlefield added fire to their beliefs. It proved to the Romans the practical success of strong, central military leadership over weak, dispersed, representative and democratic leadership.

Considering all this, it is not surprising that the Romans considered political leadership the special province of the strong, the wealthy, and the elite. But their thinking was not quite the same as that of the Egyptians, Mesopotamians, and Chinese on the subject. The important difference was that the Romans—unlike the others—did not base the authority of their rulers on any special relationship with the gods. As a result, no one had an inherent *right* to rule; leaders had to win their offices through effectiveness, strength, and practicality. This is not to say that anyone who was an effective leader could rise to the top of the political ladder. There were definite social and economic barriers to such a course, although they were occasionally overcome by particularly

The prince's main duties were providing justice and freeing roads and cities from roving criminals, according to the original caption. (By Jost Amman, from The Book of Trades, *late 16th century)*

resolute individuals, such as Cicero. What it did mean, was that, among the elite, the best qualified and most capable leaders were the ones who usually came into power. This emphasis on leaders having to prove themselves is often considered one of the major strengths of the Roman political system. The fact that its leaders had to earn their positions—and through ineffectiveness might also lose them—meant that the state would usually have at least adequate leadership.

The *emperor* either directly or indirectly appointed people to fill most other positions of political leadership. Yet the emperor was more likely to disperse his authority than had been the case with the kings of Egypt and Mesopotamia. One explanation for this behavior is that before the establishment of the Republic, Roman kings had become accustomed to consulting male heads of prominent families for advice on various matters. These *patres* (fathers) eventually came to form a distinct noble class known as the *patricians*. From this class was derived an assembly of older citizens, which was finally embodied as the Roman *Senate* (from the Latin word *senses*, meaning "old man").

In the days of the Republic, before the office of the emperor became all-powerful, the Senate was very important. *Senators* were elected annually. Because they earned no pay for doing their political duty, only wealthy and self-sufficient men could hold such a post. Only the patricians could vote, in any case, so the seemingly democratic body was really quite elite throughout the greater part of the Republic. Common citizens did obtain fuller rights as time went on, but Senators remained an elitist class. No longer necessarily elitist by birth, the men elected to the Senate became elitist simply by virtue of being members of that prestigious body.

The Senate went through periods when it was very strong, or at least was well represented by a few eloquent and influential members. It was never in total command of the Republic, however, even though it was the chief legislative body and had a strong voice in all foreign and domestic affairs. It shared the role of political leadership with the holders of some other elective positions. The *quaestor* headed the treasury and therefore had substantial authority over the specific use of public funds. The *aedile*, or *tribune*, supervised markets, food supplies, public buildings, and public spectacles. He exerted a strong leadership over merchant and commercial interests, as well as over the public use of food stores and city facilities. The *praetors* were *judges*, who served as chief interpreters of the law. There were also two *consuls*, chief *magistrates* who jointly administered the government in Rome. In effect, these consuls were the chief executives of Rome. They had considerable authority, especially in military matters, and were given equal power to avoid letting the Republic fall into the hands of a tyrannical monarch.

All of these positions of leadership had short one-year terms, minimum age qualifications, and no salary. Moreover, candidates for these posts had to run active and expensive campaigns, giving elaborate public games and feasts over which they presided in an attempt to win favor and votes. What was so attractive about these jobs? One attraction was the prestige that comes with holding a position of leadership. Another was the fortunes that could be made indirectly—and usually dishonestly—through the abuse of power. Most officials spent time in the provinces. It was there, away from the meticulous organization of Rome and the close scrutiny of senators and other officials, that these posts really paid off. Sometimes the profits were honest and well earned; Cicero, for example, worked so effectively on behalf of the Sicilians that they allowed him to purchase large stores of their grain at below-cost prices after he had returned to Rome. But most fortunes were obtained through blatant corruption and thievery. A Roman treasurer was sent to accompany each provincial governor to keep him honest. But the treasurer usually stole more than the governor, or at least they struck up an infamous partnership. Aediles and praetors also served one-year terms in the provinces, and even the consuls were obliged to govern there for at least one term. Verres, the governor of Sicily, was so steeped in graft and corruption that he was finally exiled. His was an exceptional case, however, and most officials were never even reprimanded for their profiteering.

A similar situation existed among the political leadership of the towns, although the corruption there operated at a much reduced level. Town magistrates were elected to one-year terms without pay. They did practically the same job as the great magistrate or consul of Rome, only on a smaller scale. In return for being elected to the post, the town magistrate—who was almost always a wealthy aristocrat—had to take upon himself the burden of improving the town and bestowing lavish gifts upon it. In return, the magistrate won public recognition and indirect opportunities, both honest and dishonest, to increase his fortune. The town council (*curia*) members, from among whom the candidates for magistrate were nominated, actually had to pay a fee to hold their posts. This situation obviously left little chance for ordinary laboring citizens to reach even the lowest level of political leadership.

The relatively enlightened Golden Age of Augustus opened up the period of the Roman Empire, when the emperor finally took supreme control of the state. Augustus retained many of the officials of state and allowed the Senate to continue to exist, but only in an advisory capacity. The Roman emperors brought a strong, central, unifying force to the great empire that had been torn with dissension and civil strife. But like all absolute leaders, their office was only as enlightened as the person in power and the officials he selected. A fine and highly qualified leader such as Augustus made the system appear wonderful, unencumbered as it was by conflicting sources of authority. But malicious and tyrannical emperors such as Caligula turned the situation into a nightmare, and Romans could only pray that some other sources of power would appear to temper the effects of such a reign.

For kings and queens, marriage was often a matter of state convenience, and a bethrothal like this one a political affair. (By Albrecht Dürer, early 16th century)

In essence, what developed during the empire, especially in its later years, was a system of political *patronage* (the rewarding of political supporters with jobs and other favors) that would characterize political leadership long after the fall of the empire itself. Members of the Senate, rather than acting as responsible political leaders, stumbled over each other to please the emperor. In so doing, they hoped to retain their prestigious standing in Roman society and even profit through the gifts of the gracious ruler. Therefore there were no more serious challenges to the emperor's authority from within legal channels but only occasional underground conspiracies, such as the one that had undone Julius Caesar, within secret groups of malcontents.

The East, too, was ruled by strong centralized governments. The Chinese emperor reigned supreme in all matters. Although he delegated portions of his authority to regular departments of state, his word was always the last. Only in some of the outlying territories, where local governors were far removed from direct royal contact, did the emperor's influence pale somewhat. This system of strong central leadership was in many respects beneficial to an empire that had incorporated vast territories with wide varieties of languages and cultures. Moreover, the administration of the Chinese empire advanced far beyond its time. An examination system was used to place officials in government positions based purely on merit rather than political favor. This system—drawing on scholars from virtually any social or economic class—remained an essential part of Chinese government until 1905 A.D. Most of the positions obtained through the examination system were clerical, and officials chosen in this way had only a remote possibility of obtaining great political influence or leadership. Still, this educational elite had some opportunity to shape policies.

One feature of the Chinese leadership can also be seen elsewhere in the East—notably in Japan, Korea, and India. Political leaders in the East were thought to have had a special authority mandated by heaven. But along with this authority came a considerable responsibility inherent in all positions of political leadership, and reaching its height in the highest office of emperor. Leaders were expected to provide adequate protection and prosperity for their subjects and were charged with offering the necessary stimulus for educational and religious progress.

In the West, after the fall of the Roman Empire, political leadership fell partly into the hands of a wide variety of local *chieftains* of marauding tribes that preyed on whatever was left of civilization. Leadership in such cases was based purely on military prowess.

The remains of Western civilization were politically organized by the Roman Catholic church and a handful of wealthy and powerful aristocrats. Actually the church had its earliest political rise to power in Constantinople, capital of the Byzantine (Eastern Roman) Empire.

Gradually, the church gained secular authority over all of Western Europe. While the *pope*, *bishops*, and lesser *clerics* who interpreted and administered the church's policies throughout the kingdoms of the West were not political leaders in theory, in actuality they had vast influence over affairs of state.

The medieval world was greatly disunited and subject to the raids and plundering of various "barbaric" tribes, especially before the ninth century. These included such groups as the Visigoths, Vandals, Anglo-Saxons, Huns, and Ostrogoths. The tribes themselves were united through an arrangement that they called the war-band (*Gefolge*) and that the Romans referred to as the *comitatus*. In the war-band, a political and military leader was chosen to lead the band of loyal tribemembers in attacking and exploiting likely victims. The arrangement received wide application in Scandinavia, Russia, and England. The Anglo-Saxons called such a chieftain a *hlaford*, from which the later term *lord* was directly

For monarchs, no stage of life was completely personal; here Henri II of France dies surrounded by a roomful of doctors, family, and courtiers. (By Jacques Perrissin, from Histoires des Guerres, *c. 1560)*

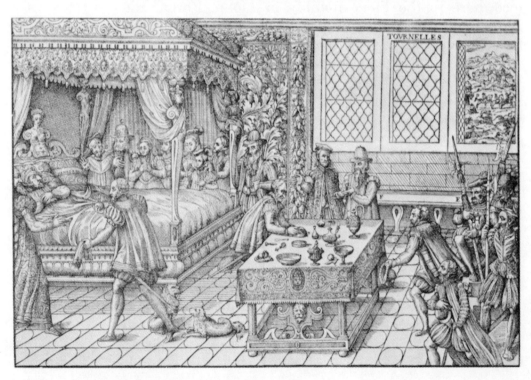

derived. The chief was typically empowered to distribute the booty fairly among his followers. Any dissatisfied members were free to join another tribe, although such dissenters often preferred to try to overthrow the chieftain and assume the title for themselves.

In defense against these tribes, powerful aristocrats created isolated *duchies* and *counties*, small political units that attempted to overcome the virtual loss of organized civilization that had come with the breakdown of the Roman Empire. Besides the aristocrats who acted as political leaders of their small communities, many church officials were appointed to such areas to assert the unifying authority of the church as much as possible. The aristocracy and the clergy often vied for political leadership within a given locality. While both feared the ever-present danger posed by disorganized, warring tribes, it was the landed aristocrats who actually began to offer protection to local people by forming small armies to withstand invasions.

Practically speaking, no central authority existed over large numbers of duchies and counties until Charlemagne ascended to the Frankish throne, after he had forged a substantial empire through military exploits. It was significant that he was crowned the "Roman Emperor" by Pope Leo III on Christmas Day, 800 A.D. The pope was apparently rewarding Charlemagne for his ardent labor in converting heathen Germanic tribes to Christianity at the point of the sword. But underlying this simple homage was the tacit implication that the Pope had such supreme authority as to name not only an emperor, but a holy one at that. This latter distinction was implicit in the term "Roman," because Rome was the capital of the holy Papal States.

Charlemagne lived up to his title by acting every bit as much a religious leader as a secular leader over his vast dominions. He did, however, attempt to undercut the secular authority of the papacy when in 813 A.D. he named his son, Louis the Pious, as his lawful successor, without consulting the pope or any other church

Absolutism and the continued inequality in British society led to sharp criticism, here of "The load borne by the British public." (By George Cruikshank, December 15, 1819)

authorities. Despite the close affection between the pope and Charlemagne, even the brilliant era of Charlemagne's rule could not mask the emerging tension between monarch and pope over the issue of secular authority. For centuries afterward, much of European history would be seen as a battleground between popes and monarchs, as each tried to assert absolute political leadership.

Still other political leaders began to appear during the reign of Charlemagne. To administer his large empire, the emperor had to appoint local governors. Since they ruled over counties, they were called *counts*. Although these positions were originally appointed by Charlemagne himself, they eventually became hereditary, thus establishing the basis for an elite class of political leaders called *nobles*. In the time of Charlemagne, though, the counts did not have the supreme authority over their districts that they eventually gained. They were charged with maintaining order, rendering justice, and recruiting and commanding soldiers. But this power was tempered by the authority of teams of judges called *scabini*, who reviewed the actions and orders of counts. As direct representatives of the emperor, the *scabini* had the power to overrule the counts. In addition, local bishops and lesser clerics also had considerable political authority, which undermined that of the counts to varying degrees.

After Charlemagne's death, his empire was carved up into smaller kingdoms. No secular ruler would establish a strong unifying force comparable to his for many centuries to come. Europe dissolved into a system of petty kingdoms and estates. The so-called age of *feudalism* represented the breakdown of secular authority, but also the rise of the pope as Europe's single most powerful political leader. During the feudal period, numerous independent little kingdoms existed in virtual isolation from one another and from the rest of the world. The only contact usually maintained between them was when they fought each other on the battlefield to settle some territorial dispute.

Political leadership over each fortressed kingdom came from the aristocrat or lord who owned the land upon which it rested and who led its citizens in forming a defensive military organization. The old word *vassus*, which had once meant a man of menial status, later came to indicate one who courageously served in the military ranks for his patron or lord. In the age of feudalism, one who rendered such military or civil service came to be known as a *vassal*. Political leadership for the remainder of the Middle Ages was wrapped up in the lord-vassal relationship. The lord provided security, protection, and a bit of prosperity for his subjects in return for the labor of the *serfs* (menial laborers) and the more prestigious service of the vassals. The lord was the main political leader of such a unit, but he delegated some of that authority to those vassals whom he chose to collect taxes, operate the army, and so forth.

The strongest and virtually only central authority that had considerable influence on and exerted definite political leadership over the kingdoms was the Catholic church. A bishop had a tremendous say in matters of state that affected his particular *diocese*. The pope, as the highest church official, had the greatest power, and was even instrumental in the success or failure that a king might expect to meet with in times of both peace and war.

An excerpt from a letter written by Pope Gregory VII in the 11th century illustrates the church's general view of the king's office:

> Who does not know that kings and rulers took their beginning from those who, being ignorant of God, have assumed, because of blind greed and intolerable presumption, to make themselves masters of their equals, namely men, by means of pride, violence, bad faith, murder, and nearly every kind of crime, being incited thereto by the prince of this world, the Devil?

Gregory was quite confident that secular government had originated in (and was too frequently perpetuated by) sin, and he was equally confident in his assertion of where political leadership ought to come from. The following statement he addressed to a council at Rome in 1080:

> So act, I beg you, holy fathers and princes, that all the world may know that, if you have power to bind and loose in Heaven, you have power on earth to take away or to grant empires, kingdoms, principalities, dukedoms, marches, counties, and the possessions of all men according to their merits...Let kings and all the princes of the world learn how great you are and what power you have and let these small men fear to disobey the command of your church.

In the 13th century, Holy Roman Emperor Frederick II, wishing to name his son as his legal successor, had to win the approval of the church by granting many privileges to bishops and abbots. He also agreed not to set up any customs stations in church territories or to build any towns or military posts on church lands. Church holdings were already free of taxation throughout Europe, and with this sort of favor it is easy to see how the church developed such tremendous political clout.

In 1237 Frederick attempted to unite all of Italy, including Rome. The Pope responded by excommunicating him in 1239 and waging a bitter battle against him. The papal military forces were eventually victorious; they killed both of Frederick II's heirs to the throne and temporarily broke up the Holy Roman Empire. (The word "Holy" had been added in the 12th century.) The papacy was clearly a formidable political as well as military force in the Western world. Its authority could be rivaled by no single leader of state for many years to come.

While the power of monarchs suffered in Europe during the Middle Ages, strong monarchies existed elsewhere in the world. In Asia—both in the Byzantine (Eastern Roman) Empire and farther east—strong emperors held tight control over their subjects, as did the *caliphs* of the Islamic world. These monarchs did not go unchallenged, however, as aristocrats in most of these lands were constantly at odds with the royal authorities. But such leaders were able to maintain a relatively strong hold on their massive empires because they generally acted as single-person leaders of both state and church. In a time when there was little concept of church-state separation, this situation was of considerable benefit to any political leader. In these parts of the world, such leadership did not break down into a disruptive, self-defeating, and bitter struggle between the monarch of the state and the leader of the church. Instead, there was a basic unity of what, in Europe, had sadly become a division of political leadership at its highest level.

Like the Byzantine and Chinese emperors, the caliphs of the Islamic world were absolute dictators. These were all political leaders of vast and expanding empires through much of the Middle Ages and centuries afterwards, even into the 20th century. They were expected to uphold the religious tenets of their respective cultures in a very active way. The caliphs led centuries of military conquest in the name of spreading the truth of Islam. The Chinese emperors were a stabilizing force over a wide diversity of Asian peoples, holding them together through a steadfast adherence to Confucian principles. In all these cases, the rulers were responsible to the citizenry for providing stable leadership. When these obligations were not handled properly, the individuals involved were replaced or overthrown by someone more effective.

In Europe, the pope remained truly the single most powerful leader of Western civilization. But even that office came under heavy criticism during the 14th century, and the church had to initiate many reforms—or at least pseudo-reforms—to improve its general image. By the middle of the 15th century the absolute power of the pope had revived fully. Yet during the two previous centuries, while the church was undergoing reform, other sources of political leadership had made significant gains. Bold aristocrats and nobles had established parliaments and free cities, which directly limited the power of monarchs and also indirectly took power away from the pope. Furthermore, the *bourgeoisie*—the wealthy merchant and business class that arose as cities developed—was also acquiring political power.

The rise in power of the aristocrats was actually an attempt to revive the declining feudal system, whereby petty lords commanded tribes of vassals and serfs with a minimum of interference by any central authority—either pope or king. But with the parallel rise of the bourgeoisie, a new dimension was added to the struggle against monarchy. This was the attempt of the urban middle class to assert its own authority through the establishment of entirely new political institutions expressly developed to act on behalf of the new society and its middle-class interests.

In England, the celebrated Magna Carta, forced upon King John in 1215, curtailed some of the monarch's power over a small and highly elite constituency of barons.

Along the same lines and perhaps of even greater lasting importance was the advisory council formed by the barons in 1258. This great council, called a *parliament*, met only three times. However, by 1295 Edward I assembled his Model Parliament that consisted not only of barons but also of *clergy*, *knights*, and *burgesses*.

In France, during the long and wasteful Hundred Years War, from 1337 to 1453, a similar council called the *Estates-General* asserted its role of political leadership. In 1357 it forced King Charles to give up his royal body of advisors and to institute, instead, a body of 28 delegates chosen from the Estates. A new political leadership was on the rise. Such movements are often hailed as the forerunners of democracy, in which the general citizenry directly elects the political representatives of its choice. However, these new political leaders were far from representing the common people. They were wealthy and independent—great landowners and successful business operators. They wanted to become political leaders, not to champion human rights but because they had high stakes at risk in the policies of government. They were, in short, serving their own interests, often to a much greater degree than enlightened monarchs did.

By the middle of the 15th century it had become apparent that the increasing size and complexity of society demanded that a greater role be played by central government. Aristocrats could never bring back a feudal society in which they were the most powerful lords of the land. Rural society now had to share some of its importance with the towns. The bourgeoisie (middle class) would find a prominent place in the new central government organizations. Sometimes this new business class provided actual rulers. The Medici in Florence, as well as the merchants of Venice and those of towns in the Hanseatic League in the north, are perfect examples of this new leadership. Sometimes the bourgeoisie assisted a monarch by providing professional skills and even capital (money) to further causes championed by the throne. The financial backing of a wealthy merchant family, the

Fuggers, for instance, was an integral part of the power of the Hapsburgs in Germany. The new bourgeois political leaders even effectively challenged the renewed power of the church. Much of this influence they gained through the appropriate use of capital. They donated money for public buildings and patronized the arts and education; they built libraries and even academies. Such was the work of the new middle-class political leader.

Still, the greatest source of political leadership in Europe at the end of the Middle Ages and even into the early modern era was the monarchy. Generally speaking, a great age of kings, of royal power, lasted from the mid-15th century to the mid-18th century. During this time Europe was transformed from a loose chain of petty kingdoms into a few strong, coherent, and centralized nations. This historical development is referred to as *nationalism*. A small number of kings became the chief political leaders of the Western world, replacing large numbers of weak, self-serving lords and aristocrats. Whether the kings came to power as a result of the rise of nationalism is unclear. Probably both phenomena worked hand in hand. What is clear is that the new nations of Europe emerged as the greatest civilizations of the world, whereas during the Middle Ages European civilization had represented backwardness and weakness.

The monarchs were closely allied to the new bourgeoisie, who were now displacing aristocrats in the government. The interests of the bourgeoisie were opposite to those of the aristocrats. The interests of the nobles were in maintaining a weak system of individual kingdoms, which they ruled. Moreover, it was important to them that the credentials for political leadership consist of land and birthright, since they possessed both. But the bourgeois rulers based their positions within government on education, training, and capital—three things that the aristocrats typically lacked.

The kings made their first moves toward establishing strong central governments by stimulating commerce and business, thus endearing themselves to the middle classes. They passed national laws making trading easier within a larger political unit. Traders no longer had to pass through a series of petty kingdoms with their own laws, transportation tolls, and customs duties. The kings also encouraged the development of cities—the centers of this new economic activity. The rise of cities further eroded the base of support that the aristocrats had long relied on. The days of isolated rural farming communities as viable economic entities were clearly coming to a close, and with it came a significant shift in political organization, institutions, and leadership.

The kings soon controlled not only the aristocrats, but the church too. Beginning in the 16th century, the Protestant Reformation greatly weakened the authority of the pope, especially in northern countries such as Germany and England, where the new commercial activity was most lively. The new *capitalists* resented the traditional church attitude that people must accept their stations in life and not try to improve upon them. They

Though Eastern leaders, like this Sultan of Sulu, received Western visitors in some states, their power was much diminished by colonialism. (From The New America and the Far East, *by G. Waldo Browne, 1901)*

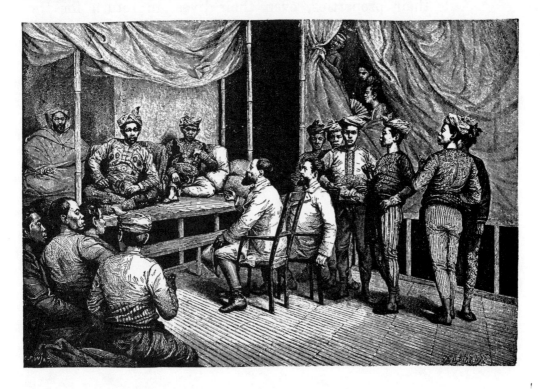

embraced instead the new *work ethic* that Protestant leaders offered. According to this belief, a person could better his station in life by working hard to show the world his fruits of God's grace. This concept shook the very base of the Roman Catholic church's authority, which had for centuries held Europeans spellbound in anticipation of God's judgment in the hereafter. Now they could go out and actively seek God's grace, not just by going to church, but by working and prospering. The new monarchs were only too willing to provide ample opportunity for this new ambition to blossom into great capitalistic ventures and generally improved economies.

National currencies (money systems), armies, and laws were all sponsored by the absolute monarchs. Their strong central governments revamped economies and brought both church leaders and aristocrats under control. Eventually, the aristocrats and some of the clergy as well would seek easy positions of pomp and prestige in the grand royal courts. They would freely offer their services, their properties, even their lives, in return for the patronage of the great kings. Even the pope himself finally saw crushing blows to his authority, beginning with Henry VIII's establishment of a national church, called the Church of England, or the Anglican church, which replaced the Roman Catholic church in England. Henry accomplished this through the Act of Supremacy of 1534, in which he defiantly stated that the king was "the only supreme head on earth of the Church of England." Elsewhere in Europe, monasteries and other church lands were taken over by monarchs, both Protestant and Catholic.

For three centuries Europe was reshaped, reorganized, and considerably strengthened by the institution of modern absolutism. If we wonder how people could have tolerated such seeming tyranny by one-person governments in the period between 1450 and 1750, we miss a significant feature of the nature of political leadership. Above all else, these rulers were empowered to deliver political stability combined with economic

prosperity. The medieval lord-and-vassal system had been effective in doing this on a local level in a world dominated by the church and its view of society, which held all people rigidly in the social and economic classes to which they had been born. But such religious and local forms of political leadership became obsolete when trade activity and towns began to grow beyond strictly local boundaries. The new middle-class merchants and manufacturers needed and demanded standardization: uniform customs rates, national monetary policies, the issuance of currency, national transportation systems and tolls, as well as national military and civil protection, and uniform laws. It was in this atmosphere of nationalistic fervor that absolute monarchs were generally welcomed as the sorely needed unifying forces of the new states. Strength and central government were wanted even at the risk of tyranny and absolutism.

Not all monarchs were evil, not all were fair; not all were strong, not all were weak. One thing can be stated

Universal suffrage has often been more a theory than a reality for minorities like these Blacks in America's South after the Civil War. (Library of Congress)

definitely about the nature of the profession of political leadership during this period: it was free to define itself. Each individual monarch made of the office whatever he or she wished or was capable of. Monarchs could do almost anything as long as they did so "in accordance with the laws of God." Since it was assumed that they ruled by divine right, it was difficult to charge them with doing anything that was not divinely ordered. Although it was only on this point of morality that the churches—both Protestant and Catholic—could challenge the monarch's authority at all, it became rather widely acceptable for a monarch to do anything to increase the strength of the state. The means used to accomplish stability and prosperity became less important to people than the ends achieved. This concept of political leadership—characteristic of the absolute monarchs of this era—is typically referred to as *Machiavellianism*.

Machiavelli's famous book *The Prince* is usually held as the best example of the standards of political leadership

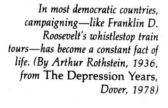

In most democratic countries, campaigning—like Franklin D. Roosevelt's whistlestop train tours—has become a constant fact of life. (By Arthur Rothstein, 1936, from The Depression Years, *Dover, 1978)*

in the early modern state. It is often claimed that Machiavelli urged monarchs to disregard morality (ideas of right and wrong) totally. This view is not quite accurate. He did, however, insist on the importance of a strong monarchy in unifying a people and their common interests. Such unity was sorely lacking in Machiavelli's homeland, Italy, which remained divided among petty aristocrats and wealthy merchants long after other countries had overcome the weak and outdated feudalistic power structure. He clearly believed that there was little more important than having a strong monarch and central government in his country and in his time. The following remarks of Machiavelli attest to this:

> In fact it is vain to look for anything good from those countries which we see nowadays so corrupt, as is the case above all others with Italy. France and Spain also have their share of corruption, and if we do not see so many disorders and troubles in those countries as is the case daily in Italy, it is not so much owing to the goodness of their people...as to the fact that they have each a king who keeps them united....

Machiavelli even supported the practice adopted by the new divine-right monarchs of assuming absolute authority to make laws:

> But we must assume, as a general rule, that it never or rarely happens that a republic or monarchy is well constituted, or its old institutions entirely reformed, unless it is done by only one individual; it is even necessary that he whose mind has conceived such a constitution should be alone in carrying it into effect.

Yet, for all the power and authority that Machiavelli was willing to concede to the monarch, he always insisted that this power—even if obtained through violence and deception (and he saw nothing wrong with that)—must not abuse the welfare of the state or its citizenry. Kings were to be granted the full powers of government, not to abuse the state, but to put an end to the weakness and corruption that the old feudal system had fostered. He makes this point clear:

> The only way to establish any kind of order there is to found a monarchical government; for where the body of the people is so thoroughly corrupt that the laws are powerless for restraint, it becomes necessary to establish some superior power which, with a royal hand, and with full and absolute powers, may put a curb upon the excessive ambition and corruption of the powerful.

The new kings, then, were freely granted absolute authority in order to put an end to the abuses of the aristocracy and clergy, and to provide a new climate for the growth of commerce. This new climate was to be found in the creation of powerful nations. The constitutional monarchs who ruled in England and France toward the end of the Middle Ages had proven too weak for such a task.

The new, more powerful monarchs included Ferdinand and Isabella, who united the kingdoms of Aragon and Castile to form the nation of Spain; it soon became the most powerful nation in the world throughout the 16th century. The new absolutism began in England with Henry VII and was strengthened by Henry VIII, even though Parliament retained some limited powers. Germany and Italy remained divided among principalities and petty kingdoms for a much longer time, not to be finally united under central rule until the 19th century. France became the supreme example of absolute monarchy. The Ordinance of 1439 gave the king total control over the military and the right to impose a national tax to support it. The Estates-General was relegated to a mere shadow of what it once had been. It could meet only with the grace and at the beckon of the king.

The history of political leadership is filled with both great monarchs and terrible monarchs. That is true of the European kings and queens, as well as of the *czars* in

Russia, the emperors of the Far East, and the caliphs of Islam. Other positions of leadership were made available within royal courts or in outlying districts at the discretion of the monarch. Sometimes close advisors became extremely influential and attained as much power as the monarch themselves. Such powerful advisors included Cardinal Richelieu and Cardinal Mazarin of France and Rasputin of Russia. Also under the king's supervision were various leaders who exercised local authority—governors, *burghers*, and *mayors*, and legislative bodies or advisory councils, as well as some members of the clergy, who still effectively governed many small towns and districts. It was from among people such as these that a new class of political leaders would eventually rise to replace most of the absolute monarchs.

For the monarchy, in the very absoluteness of its authority, began to arouse widespread resentment. Absolute monarchs had fulfilled their function of forming strong national states and of delivering them from the divisive power of aristocrats and nobles. Moreover, they had established institutions that created feelings of national fervor and cohesiveness, sentiments which could not have been developed by an international body such as the Roman Catholic church. (The long, slow separation of church and state that followed the Protestant Reformation finally put an end to the pope's designs on secular leadership.)

As states became more prosperous and cohesive, they began to find that the self-serving interests of the monarchs made the office cumbersome, counterproductive, and finally reactionary. Political instability and upheaval often ensued with each succession to the throne. (The succession of leaders to power is still a major problem faced by modern states, especially those whose leaders are not elected.)

Groups of wealthy middle-class merchants, capitalists, and intellectuals began to clamor for a voice in political leadership. Political philosophers such as Thomas Hobbes, John Locke, Jean Jacques Rousseau, and

Voltaire expressed the opinion that monarchs really had no divine right to authority, and that where their leadership was counterproductive to the economic and social needs of the state, they ought to be replaced.

Constitutional reforms began as early as the 17th century in England. Monarchs started sharing their authority with elected representatives of the general populace and eventually would concede all of their power to Parliament. In North America, colonists rebelled against the government imposed by the English monarch and, after a violent revolution, created a new nation—the United States. A federal system of government was established, with popular elections used to select political leaders ranging from town council representatives to national legislators, including (through a complicated system called the Electoral College) the president. In France, too, a revolution removed the monarch and, after several other revolutions throughout the 19th century, a representative form of government was created there. The great revolutions in Europe and North America in the 18th and 19th centuries were followed by many other lesser ones in Asia, Africa, and South America, into the current century. All were aimed at providing a government more responsive to the will of the people, with widely varying success.

After the rise of industrialism in the 19th century, and general resentment over the massive power wielded by the capitalists who controlled major industries, some popular political movements focused on sharing not only political but also economic power among the general population. Political-economic philosophers such as Karl Marx suggested that the ideal society would be one without classes, in which industry was controlled by the government, composed of all the people. Following the ideas of communism—in a wider sense, socialism—revolutions in the 20th century led to the fall of several despotic rulers, notably in Russia and China. The reality has fallen far short of the ideal, however. In the newly established Communist governments in such countries, political leaders are generally drawn from among a rather small group of people—a new political aristocracy. Influenced by socialist ideas, some countries have adopted a middle ground, nationalizing many of the major industries—that is, bringing them under the control of the nation—while keeping a general representative form of government; Great Britain has, in the late 20th century, had this mixed form of political economy.

In many countries, absolute power has been restored or retained in the form of military dictatorships. In these places, the leaders often rise to power through military strength and support. Otherwise, they act much like the absolute monarchs did. On occasion, like the kings of old, some dictators have proven to be good rulers, and have instituted important and beneficial changes in government and society, often providing much-needed stability. But many others have proven to be harshly repressive and unconcerned for the public welfare or for social or economic progress. Hitler's Germany and Mussolini's Italy were frightening examples of the lengths to which government abuse of power could be taken. Military dictatorships, often called *police states*, have been created in many Third World nations in the 20th century.

In recent decades, some communities have hired professional city managers to run their municipalities. (International City Management Association)

So in the last three centuries, political leadership in most countries has gradually been taken away from the monarchs and won over by special groups and sometimes by the citizenry in general. Because of the changing nature of government in that period, political leadership has taken on a new look. Legislators—many of them trained as *lawyers*—have become very important in democratic nations, where laws are not handed down by a central authority. Mayors of cities, town councillors, and governors of states, districts, and territories, senators, and representatives of all sorts have all gained a great deal of power within their delegated realms. In democratic nations, the process of being elected to a position of political leadership on virtually any level has become very sophisticated and complex. *Constituencies* (those people who elect leaders and to whom the leaders are responsible) now include practically every adult in such societies, where once they included only a small elite portion of the population. Political leaders in democratic countries, therefore, have had to become more responsive to the needs and demands of all classes and types of people. Laborers, women, and minorities have increasingly gained a hearing for their interests and have themselves become *politicians*.

Still at issue within the profession of political leadership is the relationship between political objectives or ends and the means employed to reach those ends. Many leaders still hold to the Machiavellian notion that any means of accomplishing power and political goals are justified by the ends of such actions—assuming that the latter are themselves just. In many countries this sort of "power politics" is well accepted and even respected. In more democratic nations, however, only moral means—those adhering to the rules and conventions of the society—are generally accepted as appropriate, regardless of the desirability of the objective. The actions of political leaders in these nations are carefully scrutinized by the public and the press. For example, former United States President Richard Nixon was forced to resign his high office because of improprieties that would hardly have raised eyebrows in a great many countries throughout the world.

At the opposite extreme are the military dictators and tyrants. These leaders have gone far beyond Machiavellianism because they disregard totally the welfare of the nations they control. During the Carter years, the United States stood behind a policy of *international human rights*, under which it refused to deal with many foreign rulers who abused their power by impinging on human rights, regardless of how proper the long-term goals of those rulers may have been. Later the Reagan administration largely undid this policy. Clearly, however, the issues related to the nature and practices of political leadership have become international in scope.

For related occupations in this volume, *Leaders and Lawyers*, see the following:
  Border Control Officials
  Inspectors
  Lawyers
  Judges
  Police and Other Law Enforcement Officers
  Secret Police

For related occupations in other volumes of the series, see the following:
in *Builders*:
  Architects and Contractors
in *Financiers and Traders*:
  Bankers and Financiers
  Merchants and Shopkeepers
in *Harvesters* (to be published Spring 1987):
  Farmers
in *Scholars and Priests* (to be published Fall 1987):
  Priests
  Scholars
in *Warriors and Adventurers* (to be published Fall 1987):
  Soldiers

Prison Guards
and Executioners

Prison guards and *head guards*, or *wardens*, are responsible for law enforcement, crime prevention, and the safety and security of the public. In these ways, they are like *police officials*, the chief difference being that they work with a special public and special rules within a controlled environment. Prison guards today are also called *correctional officers* or *correction officers*, a reflection of the hope that their relationship with the prisoners they guard will help to "correct" the prisoners' social attitudes and behavior so that they may become good citizens after they leave prison. The occupation of *warden*, head administrator of a large prison complex, derives from the old job of jail *ward* or *watch man*. The ward was responsible for simply feeding the prisoner and making sure that he could not escape until a circuit *judge* or standing court could hear his case.

Overseeing the tearful parting of convicted brother and sister, this prison guard wears a uniform much like that of an early police officer. (By George Cruikshank, from The Drunkard's Children: The Sequel to the Bottle, *1848)*

Prisons were rarely used before the mid-18th century. Those who broke the laws of society before that time were either executed, maimed, exiled, or placed in forced-labor situations, such as manning the oars of a seagoing vessel or digging in the royal mines. As a result, there were very few prisoners but many slaves and state laborers. These were overseen by harsh *slave masters*, who made sure the captives put in a good day's work. By the end of the 18th century, it had become common to house convicts in special institutions called *prisons*, in which they could be more closely guarded and better separated from society. Guards were needed to tend to the security of these prisons, *administrators* to see to their efficiency and adequacy, and *matrons* to oversee female prisoners. In some places long-term prison terms were expressly forbidden. In the Roman Empire, for example, the third-century A.D. legal scholar Ulpian noted that provincial governors should not sentence people to be held in prison: "This is illegal, since such forms of punishment have been prohibited....Prison ought to be used for detention only and not for punishment." This use of prisons as temporary holding places for people awaiting trial remained the norm—though often breached in practice—for centuries.

But in the social upheaval following the Reformation, countries such as England in the 16th century began increasingly to turn toward prisons as longer-term holding places for beggars, vagrants, and debtors, as well as accused criminals waiting trial. Such prisoners were, where no formal jail existed, simply farmed out to a local warden or *innkeeper*; these keepers extorted fees from inmates, who were obliged to pay for their board. In the absence of large prison houses, many of these prisoners were instead transported around the world to various British colonies, notably to North America and Australia.

Other European countries, too, developed institutions for those who had fallen afoul of society's rules in one way or another. Some of these were "workhouses for the poor and idle people;" others billed themselves as houses of correction or reformatories. All these had as their aim the regeneration or rehabilitation of the inmates—that is, they aimed to restore them to a useful life. These prisons required guards to tend to the security of the institutions, and administrators to oversee their efficiency and adequacy. Men, women, and children were often housed in separate institutions, or at least separate sections, and women officers, sometimes called *matrons*, often guarded inmates of their own sex.

Guards and wardens in these early prisons were known to be very harsh and inhumane. But reform movements, especially in the late 19th and early 20th centuries, have increasingly obliged them to view their jobs as more related to the rehabilitation than to the punishment of the convicted criminal—though the reality is far from the ideal. Although the modern prison is a Western invention, it has been adopted throughout the world. Many other countries have old-style harsh prison systems, in which guards and wardens are frequently military officers, who torture and abuse criminal and political prisoners alike. In this case they have retained the concept of prison as a punishment, especially when such treatment serves as an example of what may happen to opponents of the government and the state, which really controls both the penal institutions and their personnel.

While Western democracies are sometimes criticized for their supposedly soft and liberal treatment of the imprisoned, guards in these countries, too, still often abuse their power. The pressures on them have, in truth, increased steadily over recent decades, as prisons become more and more overcrowded with increasingly violent prisoners. And prison guards are truly on the front line in case of a prisoners' uprising, in which guards are often taken as hostages, sometimes losing their lives.

Closely related to the occupation of prison guard are those of *executioner* and *torturer*. Executions have been standard punishments from the earliest times we know; equally common, for lesser offenses, have been amputations. Indeed, in India, surgeons did a thriving business replacing the chopped-off noses and ears of

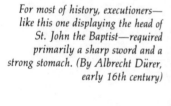

For most of history, executioners—like this one displaying the head of St. John the Baptist—required primarily a sharp sword and a strong stomach. (By Albrecht Dürer, early 16th century)

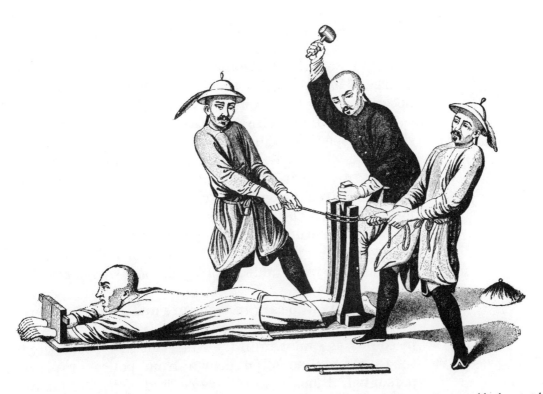

criminals with flaps of skin from elsewhere on the body. Though decapitation was a frequent punishment, some especially severe crimes in China called for the perpetrator's body to be cut in half. For even more serious crimes, the Chinese sometimes killed the rest of the immediate family as well, a practice found in various societies, though often informally. People scheduled for decapitation often tipped the *axeman* to be sure the blade was sharp, in hopes that the job—if it needed to be carried out—was completed in one stroke, rather than requiring several hacks at the neck.

Executioners lived a lonely life, for they were regarded with fear and some awe, being in frequent touch with what many regarded as the mystery of death. In Europe, the executioner often wore a face mask for anonymity or at least privacy, but in small communities, the executioner's identity was surely known, for many people would beg for pieces of the deceased's clothing or locks of hair, as points of contact with "the other side." Many axemen made a profitable sideline out of selling such items, which they were allowed to dispose of. The same conditions applied to *hangmen*—and those who were in charge of the later *guillotines*—though many of them did not cover their faces, but went dressed as to church.

Torturers have also practiced a regrettably long-standing specialty. Humans have over thousands of years devised a wide variety of means by which people can be forced to divulge information. In early modern times, new interest in technology led to the development of such masterpieces of torture as the rack and the spiked casket. In the 20th century, the development of electricity has led to a whole new generation of devices for inflicting pain, and chemistry has added more gruesome weapons to the arsenal.

The people who carry out torture and executions have often been *soldiers*; often they still are in times of war or in countries under military rule. But in modern times they are just as often drawn from police or prison personnel, though *secret police* and *spies* frequently partake of both worlds. In modern times executions are less commonly public, and the responsibility for the killing is often spread among several people. For example, a firing squad may be instructed to shoot at a targeted convict, but only one of the group has a loaded rifle, while others shoot blanks, so no one—including the shooters—knows the identity of the actual executioner. More recently, for those countries that still carry out executions, the electric chair has been used for the purpose, with injection of lethal doses of drugs becoming more common as a preferred method. In these cases, a prison guard generally operates the electric chair or a medical officer gives the injection, though some *physicians* have objected to the practice.

For related occupations in this volume, *Leaders and Lawyers*, see the following:
Police and Other Law Enforcement Officers
Secret Police

For related occupations in other volumes of the series, see the following:
in *Helpers and Aides* (to be published Spring 1987):
  Social Workers
  Undertakers
in *Healers* (to be published Spring 1987):
  Physicians and Surgeons
in *Warriors and Adventurers* (to be published Spring 1988):
  Robbers and Other Criminals
  Soldiers
  Spies

Secret Police

Secret police officers, usually employed directly through military agencies, are chiefly concerned with suppressing political opposition to their government. They typically operate secretly to secure information that will lead them to discovering people who strongly disagree with the government and apprehending suspected revolutionaries. More often than not, they use strong-arm tactics and terrorism to obtain information and make arrests, and they are frequently empowered to act as *judge, jury*, and *executioner* on an informal basis. Their authority usually supersedes that of all other law enforcement agencies.

The ancient Egyptian kings had *secret agents*, who sought out unfaithful government officials, especially those in outlying territories controlled by the pharaoh.

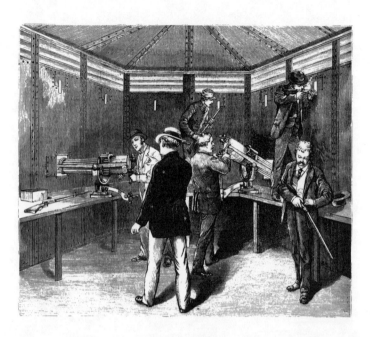

They also kept a close eye on court officials who desired radical changes or outright rebellion. The ancient Spartans in Greece and the Romans had similar officials. The *informers* or secret police of the Julian emperors in Rome were rewarded for discovering political conspiracies against the crown; they received a portion of the conspirators' confiscated estates and holdings.

Many such secret police organizations existed in the medieval world. The Council of Ten was created in 1310 A.D. to protect the city-state of Venice following an unsuccessful conspiracy against it. It added a secret police agency in 1539 that investigated moral, religious, and criminal as well as political offenses. This agency was not finally dissolved until the fall of the republic in 1797. Ivan the Terrible, czar of Russia, created a similar organization in 1565 to combat conspiracies against his regime. The so-called *oprichniki* were generously rewarded for their work in unleashing a reign of terror to protect the czar's crown. The *Vehmgericht* was a council of criminal tribunals who could act outside the law on behalf of the Holy Roman Emperor in a time of endless feudal warfare and lawlessness. The council was originally independent of the military establishment and was operated by citizen volunteers who formed "holy bands" sworn to secrecy even when faced with death or torture. Even the church Inquisitions of Rome and especially Spain used secret police organizations to build cases against suspected religious heretics—people whose beliefs differed from those of the Catholic church. Since heresy—disagreement with established church religious views—was a civil crime in medieval Europe, however, the state soon took control of both the Inquisition courts and its secret police. They often used them to investigate and prosecute political offenders under the guise of religious concern.

While most of the secret police forces in history have based their operations on terrorism, it has only been in 20th-century totalitarian states that these forces have truly earned the infamy associated with the mere mention of their names. Secret police in Russia, Germany, and the East were especially noted for their ruthlessness and their attempts to control not only the actions of citizens, but even their beliefs and thoughts. The Japanese secret police force that was dismantled at the end of World War

A government agent or secret police officer spends a great deal of time doing routine surveillance. (U. S. Department of Justice, Federal Bureau of Investigation)

II, for example, was appropriately called the Thought Police. Secret police of the Russian czar were so zealous in infiltrating revolutionary groups (including those that finally staged the successful Revolution of 1917) that they even took part in assassinations of government officials. Ironically, no sooner had the socialist revolutionaries ousted the oppressive czarist régime than they created their own secret police, called the Cheka. That organization went through several changes before 1953 when, as the MVD, it was actually ordered to arrest and execute its own director, Lavrenti Beria. Thereafter it was reorganized as the Committee of State Security—the KGB.

The most notorious of all secret police agencies in history was probably Hitler's strictly military Gestapo and SS (Schutzstaffel), whose members originally acted as his private bodyguards. These organizations not only sought out and freely executed anti-government activists or suspects but also committed crimes against humanity on a horrifying scale. Everyone knows of the extermination and concentration camps that marked their reign of terror and attempted genocide, especially of the Jewish people.

Democratic nations have typically employed secret police forces primarily for secret investigations and protection. Perhaps the best known of these organizations is the United States Secret Service. It was created in 1865 in the same year as the assassination of President Abraham Lincoln, but only to investigate currency counterfeiting. When President William McKinley was also assassinated in 1901, the agency was given the additional task for which it is now most famous—personal and family protection for the nation's president and vice-president, as well as for foreign diplomats residing in official embassies in Washington, D.C. Today they are also charged with protecting the president-elect, the vice-president-elect, major presidential and vice-presidential candidates, and former presidents and their family members. They also provide uniformed security for the

White House, the Executive Office Building, the vice-president's residence, and foreign diplomatic missions in Washington, D.C. Beyond all this, Secret Service agents still attempt to prevent currency counterfeiting as well as forgery and the fraudulent negotiation of checks, bonds, and securities.

Whether secret police personnel are military, paramilitary, or civilian, they have always been associated with the special protection of the government in power and its leaders. For this reason, they have generally enjoyed rather high prestige and excellent rewards and benefits. They have also been subjected to rigid standards of physical stature, conduct, and character as well as programs of mental, physical, and martial training. Their allegiance to the government by which they are employed must be unquestioned, and they must be willing to do virtually anything for the security of that government and the safety of its leaders. Historically, they have been called upon to terrorize, torture, and execute offenders, as well as to willingly surrender their lives if necessary to thwart an assassination attempt or to break a conspiracy against the government. Elements of all of these features are still found in the contemporary profession in a wide variety of organizations throughout the world.

For related occupations in this volume, *Leaders and Lawyers*, see the following:
    Judges
    Police and Other Law Enforcement Officers
    Political Leaders
    Prison Guards and Executioners

For related occupations in other volumes of the series, see the following:
in *Warriors and Adventurers* (to be published Spring 1988):
    Soldiers
    Spies

Suggestions for Further Reading

For further information about the occupations in this volume, you may wish to consult the books below.

Lawyers and Judges

Auerback, Jerold S. *Unequal Justice*. New York: Oxford University Press, 1976. A strong argument aimed at the failure of the legal profession to assume social responsibility in the last hundred years.

Bonner, R. J., and T. C. Burgess. *Lawyers and Litigants in Ancient Athens: Genesis of the Legal Profession*. Chicago: University of Chicago Press, 1927; 1969 reprint by Barnes and Noble. Looks at some of the earliest practitioners of the legal profession, and some standards they set for those who followed them.

Burdick, William L. *The Bench and Bar of Other Lands*. New York: S. W. Heinman, 1982; reprint of 1939 edition. A readable report on foreign legal systems, written by an American legal scholar.

Derriman, James. *Pageantry of the Law*. London: Eyre & Spottiswoode, 1955. A colorful yet informative look at the glorified, ceremonious practice of law—both bench and bar—in England and Wales.

Henke, Jack. *Lawyers and the Law in New York: A Short History and Guide*. New York: Charles Evans Hughes Press, 1979. A colorful illustrative history of the legal professions in New York, from Colonial times to the 20th century.

James, Marlise. *The People's Lawyers*. New York: Holt, Rinehart & Winston, 1973. Discusses "the radicalization of the legal profession."

Mayer, Martin. *The Lawyers*. New York: Harper & Row, 1967. An anecdotal look at all types of lawyers in modern America—"from skyscraper suite to storefront office, country courthouse to Supreme Court."

Pound, Roscoe. *The Lawyer from Antiquity to Modern Times: With Particular Reference to the Development of Bar Associations in the United States*. St. Paul, Minn.: West Publishing Co., 1953. Discusses the significance of the legal profession in the development of society; an excellent review of the historical growth and independence of the bar.

Rembar, Charles. *The Law of the Land: The Evolution of Our Legal System*. New York: Simon & Schuster, 1980. A readable, historical review of the progress of Western law and its associated occupations.

Schulz, F. *History of Roman Legal Science*. London: Oxford University Press, 1953; reprint of 1946 edition. Reviews the roles of jurists and lawyers in the Roman legal system, which set the standards for subsequent developments in the profession.

Wigmore, J. H. *Panorama of the World's Legal Systems*. Washington, D.C.: Washington Law Book Co., 1936. An excellent, time-honored, general survey of the history of law, and the professional developments of the judiciary and the bar.

Zane, John Maxcy. *The Story of Law*. New York: Ives Washburn, 1927. An excellent historical review of early developments in law and the legal professions. Mostly helpful in understanding ancient, medieval, and pre-modern developments.

Police Officers and Inspectors

Adams, Thomas F. *Law Enforcement: An Introduction to the Police Role in the Community*. Englewood Cliffs, N.J.: Prentice-Hall, 1968. A mostly contemporary look at the professional police force in the United States; includes some sections on the general historical growth of the law enforcement occupations.

Carson, Edward. *The Ancient and Rightful Customs: A History of the English Customs Service*. Hamden, Conn.: Archon Books, 1972. An intriguing review of the professions related to customs, excise, and tax collecting in all periods of British history.

Garforth, John. *A Day in the Life of a Victorian Policeman*. London: George Allen & Unwin, 1974. An extremely colorful look at the nature of the occupation in Victorian England.

Political Leaders

Harmon, Mont Judd. *Political Thought: From Plato to the Present*. New York: McGraw-Hill, 1964. A study of political ideas and their impact on history.

Sabine, George H. *A History of Political Theory*, third edition. New York: Holt, Rinehart & Winston, 1961. A broad, in-depth, and topical study of various forms, trends, and philosophies of political leadership.

Sibley, Mulford. *Political Ideas and Ideologies: A History of Political Thought*. New York: Harper & Row, 1970. A thorough treatment of the subject, with broad perspectives on political leadership throughout the ages.

INDEX

Sentencing. *See*
  Punishment
Serfs, 35, 147
Sewall, Samuel, 79
Sheriffs, 41, 107
Shires, 107
Sicily, leaders in, 140-41
Socialism, 160-61
Socrates, trial of, 58-59
Soldiers
    for border control, 1
    as customs officials,
      3
    as executioners, 42
    as judges, 42
    as police officers, 106

Solomon (King of Israel),
  20, 53
Solon, 135
Spain, balance of trade in,
  2
Sparta, 137
    government of, 133-135
    law enforcement in,
      106
Stare decicis, 48
Story, Joseph, 85-86
Strikes, 46

Sycophants, 57-58, 59

Tacitus, 60
Tariffs, 1-3. *See also*
    Customs duties
Technology, in police work,
  116
Tenures (Littleton), 40
Texas Rangers, 121
Thieves, 111
Third World, 122, 161
Torture, 30, 34-35, 167,
  168-70, 177
Trials, 75-76
    by combat, 34
    by ordeal, 33-34
Tributes, 130
Tutankhamen, 131

Union of Soviet Socialist
    Republics (U.S.S.R.)
    judges in, 50
    lawyers in, 98-99
    secret police in, 175-
      76
    socialism in, 160
U.S. Congress, as dominated
    by lawyers, 87

U.S. Marshal, 115
U.S. Supreme Court, 47, 51

Van Gulik, Robert, 29
Vassals, 147, 155
Vigilantes, 120
Vollmer, August, 118
Voltaire, Jean Francois
    Arouet, 160

War, 15
Wardens, 165
"Watch and Ward," 110
Watchmen, 107, 109, 115
Winthrop, John, 42
Work ethic, Protestant, 154
Workhouses, 167
Working class, 44, 45
Women
    as barristers, 96
    as lawyers, 51, 96
    as murderers, 114
    as police. *See*
      Policewomen
    as politicians, 162

Year Books, 37

Zenger, John Peter, 83